OZCLARKE

My top Wines for 2013

PAVILION

First published in 2012 by Pavilion Books
An imprint of
Anova Books Company Ltd
10 Southcombe Street
London W14 0RA

www.anovabooks.com

Keep up to date with Oz on his website www.ozclarke.com. Here you can find information about his books, wine recommendations, recipes, wine and food matching, event details, competitions, special offers and lots more...

Commissioning editor Fiona Holman
Editor Jamie Ambrose
Designer Georgina Hewitt
Editorial assistants Charlotte Selby, Jessica Selby

A CIP catalogue for this book is available from the British Library
ISBN 978-1-862-059696

10 9 8 7 6 5 4 3 2 1
Printed and bound in Italy by G. Canale & C.SpA

The information and prices contained in this book were correct to the best of our knowledge when we went to press. Although every care has been taken in the preparation of this book, neither the publishers nor the editors can accept any liability for any consequences arising from the use of information contained herein.

Oz Clarke My Top Wines for 2013 is an annual wine buying guide. We welcome any suggestions you might have for the next edition.

Acknowledgements

We would like to thank all the retailers, agents and individuals who have provided tasting samples and helped to source wine labels and bottle photographs.

Prices are subject to change. All prices listed are per 75cl bottle inclusive of VAT, unless otherwise stated. Remember that some retailers only sell by the case – which may be mixed. Please bear in mind that wine is not made in infinite quantities – some of these may well sell out, but the following year's vintage should then become available.

contents

introduction

God bless BBC Radio 4. When they decided to hold a poll to find out what people most liked about their radio station – with all its politics and current affairs, its music and cricket, *Desert Island Discs*, *Woman's Hour* and *The Archers* – what was the third favourite sound of the audience? **It was the sound of wine tasting**. It's not that they do much wine tasting on Radio 4, but whenever the sniff, gurgle and swallow, followed normally by 'Mmms' and 'goshes' and 'lovelys' – even 'Can I have some mores' – did come onto the airwaves, all over Britain, the volume dial was being turned up.

Was it people just laughing at the absurdity of wine tasting – especially when you couldn't see the people doing it, let alone taste the liquid itself? I don't think so. Whenever I've done radio wine tastings, firstly we've made sure that those most evocative of all sounds – **the pop of the cork and the glug glug of pouring** – are done live right next to the microphone, and I can feel the Pavlovian response of eyes brightening and lips being licked in a million homes. But, more importantly, the whole studio is abuzz with excitement. After a gruelling morning of political interviews, financial meltdowns and the search for our next Wimbledon singles champion, suddenly we're all going to have some fun. And the audience gets that. This is the truth of what wine is all about: **it's about having a laugh, discovering flavours, sharing them with others, getting a bit of a party going**. All of us feeling happier in our skins. And a good bottle of wine will do this better than a bad one.

But how good is 'good'? How do you decide? Who decides? What is 'good'? And what is 'best'? I'm not alone in thinking that we're suffering from a plague of pan-flation in many areas of British life. *The Economist*, earlier this year, took Britain to task about the fact that a British pair of size 14 women's trousers is now more than four inches wider than it was in the 1970s, when it used to be labelled size 18. Today's slimline size 10 is really a size 14.

Durham University calculated that the percentage of British kids getting 'A' grades at A-level has risen from nine to 27 per cent in 25 years, despite other tests showing that kids today aren't any cleverer than they were. The point of all this inflation – of trouser sizes, exam marks, takeaway coffee-cup sizes... oh, all that – is that it's there to make the consumer feel superficially better, but at the same time it actually devalues the whole concept.

And nowhere is this more important than where a mark is given out of 100, implying that 100 is the best there can be, the *perfecto*. As you inflate the marks below 100, you compress all the marks into a smaller and smaller space. I've been privately marking wines, either out of 20 or out of 100 for years. I admit there has been a vast improvement in wines at the lower end of the scale, and a reduction in the number I used to mark 'AE' (auto-eject) or 'DNPIM (Do Not Put In Mouth). At the top end, **while there are definitely far more examples of really exciting wines than there used to be**, I'm not sure that the 'best' are any more exciting than they were 10 or 15 years ago. Yet the marks relentlessly trend upwards. Eighty-five out of a 100 used to mean 'pretty nice stuff, interesting, enjoyable, I'll buy that'. Eighty-nine out of 100 used to mean 'really good, just off the top tier but with lots of character, definitely worth buying'. A 90/100 and you were talking a Premier League tot. That 90 has now become a 95, that 89 has now become 92-93. But 100 remains 100. No one marks out of 110.

And there's more. Does 100 points mean perfection, or doesn't it? If it does, how often in our lives do we come across perfection? In art, in music, in a dish of oysters or in a summer sky? How often in a year? Or in a day? Any wine critic now publishing scores internationally has been forced to inflate them, because not to do so, far from making readers feel reassured that they're getting good critical advice, actually makes them more unsure of themselves. If your chosen critic scores most of his wines below 90, while the next critic is mostly between 90 and 95, you feel better, more secure, following the second critic, buying his recommendations and so you subscribe to that magazine, that website, that blog. The first critic, feeling left behind and vulnerable, then joins the herd that forces as many marks as possible over 90, as many of those as possible over 95, and, once the Gadarene hysteria takes hold, the citadel of perfection is breached, perhaps once, then twice, then 19 times. Nineteen perfect wines: that's what the American *über*-critic Robert Parker awarded to the 2009 Bordeaux vintage. I haven't had 19 perfect wines in my whole life. In fact, **I don't think I know what a perfect wine is.** Nor does the great wine consultant Michel Rolland: 'I don't like to say "perfect wine",' he says, 'because perfect is always for the next wine, not the wine already done.' But in a way, Parker is hoist with his own petard. He's the one who started this marking out of 100 malarkey. If he wanted to keep lauding ever-finer vintages – and there's a lot of evidence of increasing excellence across the board in current Bordeaux – if he really thinks that 2009 is that much better than 2005, or 2000 or 1990... what's he gonna do? Turn it up to 101? Because at this rate, a better vintage than 2009 is just around the corner.

Maybe all these critics are listening to the wrong kind of music. No, I mean it. Oxford University has come out with research that demonstrates that what we listen to affects how we taste and smell, and different flavours can respond to and resemble different musical styles and instruments in our brains. Smoky and woody flavours are related to lower-pitched music. Blackberry and raspberry to the piano, vanilla more to woodwind. In one experiment, volunteers were given pieces of the same toffee to eat. They rated the toffee they ate while listening to sombre, low-pitched brass instruments as much more bitter than the toffee they ate listening to higher-pitched piano music. Same toffee, of course. Perhaps we could deal with mark inflation in the 100-point scale by flooding all the tasting rooms with recordings of the

Brigade of Guards' brass band playing the 'Dead March' from Handel's *Saul*. Well, that would be better than relying on the Drinkify.org website to reduce their scores. This website has the admirable intention of matching alcohol with music. But when it suggested recently that Britain's most popular drink ought to be the Rihanna: equal parts Red Bull, Tabasco and lemon sour, listening to the aforesaid R, I thought, 'No.'

Am I being frivolous? Well, yes. But the 100-point scale was invented to tell people what was right and what was wrong. And 'right' means getting at least 90 or ideally 95 points. So everyone – critic, retailer, consultant, producer, owner – has an interest in cramming themselves into this overstuffed top drawer and saying, 'I am the right choice. Look no further.' That should be the language of massive brands like Blossom Hill or E&J Gallo: the ones that buy loyalty with tens of millions of dollars in advertising and marketing. Right and wrong don't fit comfortably with **real wine pleasure** and true wine appreciation. Opinion fits; differences of opinion, definitely. Discussions, minds being changed, the discovery of qualities you didn't see and someone else did – and vice versa; the end of the bottle, so what did we think? Another bottle? No, something different – who's turn to choose? That's more like it. **One of the great joys of wine lies in good-natured differences of opinion.**

And **while I want you to enjoy the wines I've chosen for this guide**, I'm happy if you beg to differ, and I can't really tell you how many points they'd get out of 100, because that's not how I judged them in my tastings. I was thinking, 'What pleasure will they give? Will a white Burgundy-lover like this one, a Shiraz devotee that one? This is good value for its flavours, that one's completely mad, I have to have it in... Wow, here's a classic...' Could I mark this out of 100? I could. But I won't. I don't want to tell you what's right and wrong.

I just want to throw a whole bunch of my ideas up in the air, hoping that you'll try some of them, and be all the **happier** for it.

wine finder

CANADA
Sweet
Icewine, Gold Oak Aged Vidal, Inniskillin, Niagara Peninsula VQA, Ontario 130

CHILE
White
Chardonnay (Chilean), Morrisons, Valle Central 94

Chardonnay, The Society's Chilean, Marcelo Papa & Ignacio Recabarren, Limarí Valley 82

Chardonnay, Wild Ferment, Errázuriz, Casablanca Valley 26

Sauvignon Blanc, Indo, Anakena, San Antonio Valley 66

Red
Cabernet Sauvignon, 35° South, Viña San Pedro, Molina 88

Cabernet Sauvignon, Peñalolen, Domus Aurea, Maipo Valley 50

Carmenère, Averys Project Winemaker/Viña Casa Silva, Colchagua Valley 75

Cinsault, Viejas Tinajas, De Martino 46

Pinot Noir, Nostros Reserva, Viña Indomita, Casablanca Valley 87

Pinot Noir, Ona Single Vineyard, Anakena, Leyda Valley 71

Syrah, Corralillo, Matetic Vineyards, San Antonio Valley 42

Syrah Reserva, Aymura, Geo Wines, Elquí Valley 45

Syrah Reserva, Viña Mayu, Elquí Valley 54

Rosé
Carmenère/Syrah, Viña Mayu, Elquí Valley 102

CROATIA
White
Malvazija Istarska, Elido Pilato, Lašicí, Istria Peninsula 25

Pinot Grigio, Viña Laguna, Agrolaguna, Istria 65

ENGLAND
White
Pinot Blanc, Stopham Estate, West Sussex 23

Sparkling
Blanc de Blancs Brut, Marksman, Ridgeview Wine Estate, West Sussex 114

Gusbourne Blanc de Blancs, English Sparkling Wine, Gusbourne Estate, Kent 111

Nyetimber Classic Cuvée Sparkling Wine, Nyetimber, West Sussex 111

FRANCE
White
Bourgogne Chardonnay 'Back to the Roots', Domaine René Lequin-Colin, Burgundy 37

Bourgogne Tonnerre Blanc, Domaine de l'Abbaye du Petit Quincy, Dominique Gruhier, Burgundy 30

Burgundy, Grand Vin de Bourgogne 33

Chablis, Domaine William Fèvre, Burgundy 26

Chablis, Premier Cru, Domaine Alain Geoffroy, Burgundy 22

Chardonnay, Henri de Lorgère, Mâcon-Villages, Burgundy 94

Chardonnay, Limoux, Domaine de l'Aigle, Gérard Bertrand, Languedoc 66

Chardonnay, Le Manoir du Baron, VdP d'Oc, Foncalieu/ Domaine de Cornielle, 82

Chardonnay, L'Oeuvre de Perraud, Domaine Perraud, Mâcon-Villages, Burgundy 60

Chardonnay, Mâcon-Villages Cave de Lugny, Burgundy 82

Chardonnay/Viognier, Vignes de Nicole, IGP d'Oc, Château de Conas/Domaines Paul Mas, 63

Chat-en-Oeuf Blanc, VdP d'Oc, Boutinot, Languedoc 84

Côtes de Gascogne, Harmonie de Gascogne, Domaine de Pellehaut, Southwest France 85

Côtes de St-Mont, Le Passé Authentique, Plaimont Producteurs, Southwest France 63

Domaine Coteau de la Biche Vouvray Sec, Domaine Pichot, Loire Valley 31

Graves Albertine Peyri, Ch. Beauregard Ducasse, Bordeaux 29

Mâcon-Loché, Domaine Cordier Père et Fils, Burgundy 24

Mâcon-Verzé, Domaine Leflaive, Mâcon-Villages, Burgundy 32

Grenache Rosé, VdP des
  Coteaux de l'Ardèche, Luc
  Talleron, 103
Les Estivales, Les Vignobles
  Foncalieu/Domaine de
  Corneille, Languedoc 101
Mirabeau, Côtes de Provence,
  Provence 101
MiP – Made in Provence, Côtes de
  Provence, Domaine Sainte Lucie,
  Michel Fabre, Provence 100
Sparkling
Champagne Alexandre Bonnet,
  Brut Rosé 112
Champagne Delamotte
  Brut 113
Champagne Henri Giraud,
  Esprit Brut, Henri Giraud 111
Champagne Herbert Beaufort,
  Bouzy Grand Cru Brut 110
Champagne Jacquart Brut
  Mosaïque 113
Champagne Le Mesnil,
  Blanc de Blancs, Grand Cru
  Brut 110
Crémant de Limoux Brut,
  Cuvée Royale, Limoux 116
Premier Cru Champagne
  Brut, Tesco Finest, Union
  Champagne 114
The Society's Champagne,
  Private Cuvée, Brut, Alfred
  Gratien 112
Sparkling Burgundy Blanc
  de Blancs, Crémant de
  Bourgogne, Cave de Lugny,
  Burgundy 116

Sweet
Rivesaltes Ambré Hors d'Age,
  Arnaud de Villeneuve,
  Roussillon 132

Sauternes, Tesco Finest,
  Yvon Mau, Sauternes,
  Bordeaux 132

GEORGIA
White
Chinuri Georgian Bio Wine,
  Iago's Wine, Chardakhi 24

GERMANY
White
Riesling, Theodorus, Pfalz 31

GREECE
White
Atlantis White, Estate Argyros,
  Santorini 35
Semeli, Mantinia Nasiakos,
  Mantinia 37
Sweet
Samos Anthemis, Vin de
  Liqueur, Samos 135

HUNGARY
White
Pinot Grigio, Mátra
  Mountain 84
Tokaji Furmint, Holdvölgy
  Meditation, Moonvalley Wines,
  Tokaj 27
Rosé
Cabernet Rosé, Nagyréde
  Estate, Mátra 103

ITALY
White
Anselmi San Vincenzo, Roberto
  Anselmi, Veneto 21
Anthilia, Donnafugata,
  Sicily 28
Catarratto, Casa Lella, Araldica
  Vini Piemontesi, Sicily 86

Cortese Piemonte,
  Araldica Vini Piemontesi,
  Piedmont 86
Falanghina, Rocca Vecchia,
  Puglia 83
Falanghina, Via del Campo,
  Quintodecimo, Campania 32
Garganega, Saveroni,
  Cantina di Valpantena,
  Veneto 83
Italian Vino da Tavola Bianco,
  MGM, Mondo del Vino 95
Simply Pinot Grigio, Delle
  Venezie IGT, Cavit,
  Trento 94
Soave, Pieropan, Veneto 28
Vermentino, Collo di Luni,
  Cantine Lunae, Liguria 27
Vernaccia di San Gimignano,
  Principe Strozzi, Tuscany 33

Red
Barolo Bussia, Giacomo
  Fenocchio, Piedmont 38
Chianti Classico, Querciabella,
  Tuscany 50
Chianti Colli Senesi, Salcheto,
  Tuscany 69
Dolcetto d'Alba, Bricco
  dell'Oriolo, Azelia/Luigi
  Scavino, Piedmont 51
Langhe Nebbiolo, Sottimano,
  Piedmont 52
Montepulciano d'Abruzzo,
  Umani Ronchi, Abruzzo 89
Negroamaro, Feudi di San
  Marzano, Puglia 87
Nero d'Avola di Sicilia,
  Santa Cecilia, Planeta,
  Sicily 40
Tassinaia, Castello del
  Terriccio, Tuscany 46

Teroldego (Tesco Finest),
Vigneti delle Dolomiti,
Trento 77
Rosé
Nero d'Avola Rosato, Il
Papavero, MGM Mondo del
Vino, Sicily 102
Sparkling
Prosecco, Bisol, Veneto 116
Valdobbiadene Prosecco
Superiore, Sorelle Branca,
Veneto 115
Valdobbiadene Prosecco
Superiore, Veneto 117
Sweet
Passito di Pantelleria
Liquoroso, Pellegrino,
Sicily 134
Picolit, Colli Orientali del
Friuli, Valbene, Paolo Valle
& Alessandro Gallici, Friuli
Venezia-Giulia 131
Fortified
Marsala Riserva Dolce 5-year-
old, Martinez, Sicily 127

NEW ZEALAND
White
Blondie, Wooing Tree, Central
Otago 24
Gewurztraminer, Zephyr,
Glover Family Vineyards,
Marlborough 32
Riesling, Seifried Estate,
Nelson 61
Riesling, Waipara West,
Waipara 21
Sauvignon Blanc, Black Label,
Yealands Estate, Awatere
Valley, Marlborough 62
Sauvignon Blanc, Cape Crest,
Te Mata, Hawke's Bay 20

Sauvignon Blanc, Cellar
Selection, Villa Maria,
Marlborough 34
Sauvignon Blanc, Cowrie Bay
Marlborough 82
Sauvignon Blanc, McNaught
& Walker, Awatere Valley,
Marlborough 22
Sauvignon Blanc, Sacred Hill,
Marlborough 85
Red
Pinot Noir, Eradus,
Marlborough 40
Pinot Noir, Peregrine,
Central Otago 49
Pinot Noir (Tesco Finest),
Jenny Dobson, Central
Otago 56
Syrah, Private Bin, Villa Maria
Hawkes Bay 50
Syrah, Steam Wharf Road, Tin
Pot Hut, Hawke's Bay 43
Syrah, Woodthorpe Vineyard,
Te Mata Estate, Hawke's
Bay 39
Sparkling
Pelorus Brut, Cloudy Bay,
Marlborough 115
Sweet
Late Harvest Riesling, Waipara
West, Waipara 132

PORTUGAL
White
Dão Branco, Julia Kemper 29
Pé Branco, Herdade do
Esporão, Alentejo 83
Vinho Verde, Quinta de Azevedo,
Sogrape, Minho 68
Red
Dão, Giesta, Quinta da
Giesta 74

Douro Red, Quinta do
Crasto 72
Vinho Regional
Lisboa Tinto, Quinta de
Chocapalha, Castelão 43
Shiraz/Trincadeira,
Tagus Creek, Falua
Sociedade de Vinhos,
Alentejo 90
Fortified
Crusted Port, Graham's 124
Fonseca Terra Prima Reserve
Port from Organically
Grown Grapes, Fonseca
Guimaraens 125
Late Bottled Vintage
Unfiltered, Fonseca
Guimaraens 126
Madeira Bual 15-year-old,
Henriques & Henriques 127
Quinta dos Malvedos Vintage
Port, W & J Graham 123
Taylor's Vargellas Vintage
Port, Taylor, Fladgate &
Yeatman 123
Vintage Port, Fonseca
Guimaraens 124

ROMANIA
White
Tămâioasă Românesca Sec,
Prince Stirbey, Dealurile
Olteniei 37
Red
Pinot Noir (Sainsbury's House),
Cramele Recas 96

SOUTH AFRICA
White
Chardonnay/Semillon/Viognier,
Winifred, De Grendel,
Tygerberg 60

wine finder – country index

Chenin Blanc Reserve, Land of Hope, The Winery of Good Hope, Stellenbosch 28

Chenin Blanc, Unfiltered Terroir Selection, Springfontein Estate, Walker Bay 30

Rustenberg SWB, Rustenberg, Stellenbosch 64

Sauvignon Blanc, Iona, Elgin 29

Sauvignon Blanc, Zoetendal, Elim 64

Viognier, Ridgeback, Paarl 35

Red

John X Merriman, Rustenberg, Stellenbosch 54

Pinotage, Origin Wines, Western Cape 96

Shiraz/Cabernet Sauvignon, Cape Quarter, Overhex, Western Cape 89

Sweet

Noble Late Harvest Sauvignon Blanc, Mulderbosch, Stellenbosch 131

SPAIN
White

Albariño, Eiral, Bodegas Pablo Padin, Rías Baixas, Galicia 60

Albariño, Martín Códax, Rías Baixas, Galicia 30

Garnacha Blancha, La Miranda de Secastilla, Somontano, Aragón 61

Sauvignon Blanc, Rueda, Sitios de Bodega (Richard Sanz), Castilla y León 83

Txomín Etxaníz Getaria (Txakolí), Getariako Txakolina, País Vasco 34

Verdejo, Rueda, Casa del

Monte, Castilla y León 84

Verdejo, Rueda, Finca Montepedroso, Castilla y León 62

Viña Sol, Torres, Cataluña 84

Red

Garnacha Tinto, Cruz de Piedra, Calatayud, Aragón 91

El Guia Tinto, Bodegas Borsao, Utiel-Requena, Valencia 96

Priorat, Cartoixa, Scala Dei, Cataluña 49

Priorat Salmos, Torres, Cataluña 46

Rioja Crianza, Paco García, Rioja 71

Rioja Joven, Single Vineyard, 100% Garnacha, Averys Project Winemaker/Bodegas Medievo, Rioja 75

Rioja Reserva, Baron Amarillo, Rioja 89

Sangre de Toro, Torres, Cataluña 91

Toro Vino Tinto Joven, El Pícaro, Matsu, Toro, Castilla y León 76

Viña Alberdi Reserva, La Rioja Alta, Rioja 38

Rosé

Garnacha Rosé (Tesco Finest), Bodegas Príncipe De Viana, Navarra 102

Rioja Rosado, Muga, Rioja 100

Rosé, Toro Loco, Utiel-Requena, Valencia 103

Sparkling

Cava Brut, Metodo Tradicional, Penedès, Cataluña 117

Cava Rosado, Metodo Tradicional, Penedès, Cataluña 117

Sweet

Moscatel de Valencia, Cheste Agraria, Valencia 135

Floralis Moscatel Oro, Torres, Penedès, Cataluña 134

Fortified

Delicado Fino Sherry, González Byass 120 Dry Oloroso Sherry, Solera Jerezana, Emilio Lustau 120

Dry Old Palo Cortado, Emilio Lustau 120

Fino (The Society's), Sánchez Romate 122

Manzanilla Sherry, Williams & Humbert 121

Special Reserve Manzanilla (Tesco Finest), Bodegas Barbadilloa 121

Special Reserve Oloroso (Tesco Finest), Bodegas Barbadillo 122

TURKEY
White

Sauvignon Blanc, Sevilen, Florent Dumeau, Aegean Region 36

Red

Kalecik Karasi, Vinkara, Anatolia 73

USA
Red

Pinot Noir, Domaine Drouhin, Willamette Valley, Oregon 48

Petit Verdot, Monticello, Paul Shaffer, Second Edition, Veritas Vineyard, Virginia 44

Syrah, Charles Smith, Columbia Valley, Washington State 72

My top Wines for 2013

94

95

96

97

98

99

top 100

Looking at this array of sumptuous wines, I keep reminding myself how lucky we are in this country. Wine producers all over the world still regard Britain as the place they want their wines on show. This is despite difficult exchange-rate conditions with places like Australia and New Zealand, and rapacious behaviour on the behalf of some of our biggest retailers which makes some winemakers say it simply isn't worth trying to do business here. Yet a far greater number think it *is* worth it – and the statistics of our drinking habits prove it. Volume has faltered this year after a long, uplifting period of growth. But the number of people buying more expensive wine seems to have risen – or the same number are buying more bottles of better wine than before, often from independents or the web-based companies that are springing up all round the nation. When times are tough, we need to cheer ourselves up more than ever. Big purchases may have to wait, but spending a few pounds more on some better wine with which to mull over events and lick our wounds isn't a bad way to remind ourselves that things can only get better. This selection is here to help: 100 wines I've chosen because they lifted my spirits, brought a spring to my step and a glint into my eye. One hundred wines that made me smile, sometimes chortle with surprise and delight. One hundred wines bursting with flavour and character, sometimes from places and grapes I know well, sometimes from places and grapes I can hardly pronounce, let alone pretend to know much about. But they all give pleasure through fabulous flavours you'll remember long after you've swallowed the last drop.

• In this section you will find white wines first, then reds, listed in my preferred order.

MY TOP 50 WHITE WINES

1 **2011 Chardonnay, Reserve Release, De Bortoli, Yarra Valley, Victoria, Australia, 12.5% abv**

Planet of the Grapes, £22.50
The rehabilitation of Aussie Chardie continues in leaps and bounds. There was a time, almost a generation ago, when the big, honeyed, oaky, golden Chardies were a treasure trove for Brits starved for aeons of ripeness in our wines. But as the global wine-producing behemoths ruthlessly exploited Chardonnay's forgiving nature and hacked the neck off the golden goose, Australia's reputation went into freefall. Luckily there were enough bloody-minded Aussies out there to realize Oz had too much invested in Chardonnay to let it burn and crash. And they've been pumping

out beauties in the last few years. This is fantastic stuff: the restraint of Burgundy and the exuberance of Australia rolled into one. It smells enticingly of lemon, biscuit and hazelnuts with a fascinating savoury touch of sausage meat. The savoury quality runs right through the wine, as oatmeal, cashews, lemon zest and green apple juice provide the core of the flavours, but the final aftertaste is fresh and meaty – like the very first second a plump pork chop touches a red-hot grill.

2 **2010 Sauvignon Blanc, Cape Crest, Te Mata, Hawke's Bay, New Zealand, 13.5% abv**

Majestic, £19.99
John Buck has been making Cape Crest barrel-fermented Sauvignon for decades (I've got tasting notes going back to the 1980s) but I don't think he has ever produced a better example than this. The use of oak is amazingly subtle but adds a baked-custard and hazelnut-whip creaminess to the wine, brilliantly complementing the juicy passion fruit and nectarine that run riot through it. It gets better and better after it has been opened a while: really ripe grapefruit joins the fruit medley,

chopped hazelnuts get sprinkled on the custard cream, and somewhere a single leaf of mint just makes its presence felt.

3 2002 Riesling, Waipara West, Waipara, New Zealand, 12.5% abv

Waterloo Wine Company, £8.70

Did I read the vintage right: 2002? Yup, it seems I did. And did I read the price right: £8.70? Don't ask me how Waterloo Wines has managed this, just dash down there and buy whatever they've got. Australian Rieslings are famous for transforming from pale, sharp, citrussy youth to a golden maturity that honestly tastes like melted butter on toast and crumpets. I've never seen a New Zealand example age in the same way – but here it is, smelling of warm toast and butter and citrus zest as well as glistening, chilly rock dust.

4 2011 Anselmi San Vincenzo, Roberto Anselmi, Veneto, Italy, 13% abv

Great Western Wine, £11.95

Anselmi used to be the guiding light of Soave wine, but he increasingly found that local restrictions were preventing him from expressing his full creativity, so he gave up using 'Soave' on his label, and it's their loss, not his. Anselmi wines have never been better. This is wonderfully original wine, smelling of ripe russet apples, baked pears and savoury custard and tasting of pear and pineapple syrup that's rich but doesn't cloy and is cut by a spritzy tingle and the acid of boiled lemons and russet apple peel. But there's more, if you linger: a fern-like herb aroma, a kind of celestial boiled honey and fruit lozenge, some quince and crab-apple jelly. The longer you linger, the more you'll find.

5 2005 Semillon, Margaret, Peter Lehmann, Barossa, South Australia, 11.5% abv

Vin du Van, £14.25

Peter Lehmann named this in honour of his wife, Margaret, so it had better be good or he won't be getting any dinner. Luckily it's always a beauty. And it'll age for an awful lot longer than the seven years this one has had. We're in the astonishing world of mature Semillon: custard and buttered-toast richness scratched by wood bark, snapped awake by orange and grapefruit zest, soothed by roasted hazelnut and barely bruised by their husks.

6 2010 Sauvignon Blanc, McNaught & Walker, Awatere Valley, Marlborough, New Zealand, 13.5% abv

Private Cellar, £15.25

If you don't like Sauvignon Blancs to taste sharp and green and crunchy enough to take the gloss off your lips – well, move on to the next wine in the list. Because this one comes from Awatere, the coolest, windiest part of Marlborough in New Zealand's South Island, and it gives you both barrels of everything green. That said, the wine is surprisingly rich, and enormously improves with a bit of air – which will reveal a riot of gooseberry and green pepper, snow peas, tomato leaf, blackcurrant leaf and lime that I find irresistible.

7 2010 Chablis Premier Cru, Domaine Alain Geoffroy, Burgundy, France, 13% abv

Harvey Nichols, £22

Do you want a taste of honey in your Chablis? And can honey be dry, devoid of sweetness? Obviously it can be, because this Chablis is sensationally honeyed, yet dry as bones. It starts with the honey of acacia blossom and finishes with the heather honey

of the Scottish Highlands. And yet it is divinely speared by lemon acid, rubbed with chalk – and dry. This wine demonstrates how *premier cru* (First Growth) Chablis vineyards are better than the general run, and offer a natural extra ripeness and weight. There are many ways to make Chablis seem artificially richer, and all spoil the austere beauty of the Chablis style. M. Geoffroy grew wonderful grapes, picked them and fermented them. No interventions. Simple, really.

8 2009 Riesling Réserve, Trimbach, Alsace, France, 13.5% abv

Great Western Wine, £18.50

This wine from the Trimbach family in Alsace made it into the guide last year, too. 'Licking stones' I scrawled across the top of my tasting note. I don't expect you to get down on your knees and give it a go. But when you taste this wine, you might try to imagine that you are licking warm, dry stones smeared with honey and squirted with lime. There is a real mineral quality to this

Riesling (as indeed there should be), almost a mineral saltiness, and it's ably supported by lime juice, lemon zest and honey: ripeness and Riesling reserve in perfect balance.

9 2010 Semillon, Tim Adams, Clare Valley, South Australia, 13% abv

AustralianWineCentre.co.uk, Tesco, £11.50

Tim Adams is one of the great white-winemakers in Australia – but he doesn't like Chardonnay. Never did, never will. So he misses out on the easy sale and treads the tougher road of making great Semillon and that means making a wine with wild, unexpected flavours. Semillon often has a taste and texture like lanolin, an aroma a bit like fish oil, an acidity like lemon pith and apple peel. If that sounds a bit severe, I promise you: it works. And that's not all. There's a boiled lemon-sweet acid and ripe, almost chewy, fruit that's cosily wrapped in savoury cream and singed rice-pudding oak.

• You should also try the **Tim Adams Riesling** (AustralianWineCentre.co.uk, Tesco £10.50) for a top interpretation of that grape from a top guy.

10 2010 Pinot Blanc, Stopham Estate, West Sussex, England, 10.5% abv

Liberty Wines, £14.99, Vinoteca, £14.50

This is an historic moment. The first time I have ever put an English wine, red or white, in my top 10. And I'm thrilled. It shows that England won't merely be fizz heaven in coming years. Beautiful, ethereal, tantalizingly tasty whites are on the way as well. This isn't even from a hot year. Remember the 2010 summer? I do; I got mildew behind my ears it was so poor. But on the Arun River in West Sussex a new star arose – Stopham – and this is as good a Pinot Blanc as you'll find anywhere: elegant, delicate, with light apple fruit, a streak of springtime sap and an aroma of hedgerow blossom, with a transparent coating of crème fraîche. It's only 10.5% alcohol – and the wine gets better the longer you open it.

11 2011 Blondie, Wooing Tree, Central Otago, New Zealand, 13.5% abv

Lea & Sandeman, £22.50

This *blanc de noir* wine is made from black grapes that would normally go into Wooing Tree's hard-to-find Central Otago Pinot Noir red, so they took a risk using the fruit for a white. But it's a triumph. Lush texture, honey and lemon zest in a creamy apple purée with the odd peach and strawberry lobbed in, and a distant memory of minerals left trailing on your tongue. This tastes as though it could have made a sensational *blanc de noir* fizz, but until that happens, this is a bubble-less beauty.

12 2010 Mâcon-Loché, Domaine Cordier Père et Fils, Burgundy, France, 13.5% abv

Domaine Direct, £17-£15

There was a time, not long ago, when you'd go to Mâcon for a cheap white Burgundy, accepting that it wouldn't taste like the smart stuff. Now an increasing number of producers are making fantastically smart wine – more expensive, sure, but half the price of a decent Meursault. In fact, this tastes like Meursault: a lovely, savoury sausage-meat and oatmeal aroma and a flavour of cashews and oatmeal, peaches and Cox's apples just dabbed with lemon juice.

13 2009 Chinuri Georgian Bio Wine, Iago's Wine, Chardakhi, Georgia, 13.25% abv

Les Caves de Pyrène, £14.99

This is a 'don't say I didn't warn you' wine. Even the label gives you some idea. 'Strong aroma combined with very pleasant taste of sourness', it says. 'The wine is very deep and discloses itself with every other gulp'. You need the gulp in between, presumably, to recover from each disclosure. Well, the grapes were foot-trodden in a hollowed-out log, and then fermented and aged in earthenware amphorae. So... it's bizarre and brilliant, scented with incense and cinnamon and beeswax candles with an undertow of old banisters and staircases. And the fruit? It *is* there, but it's old, tired, like medlars, like forgotten golden-gage plums, chewy, dried-out peach skins, and a hint of honey smeared on the leather reins of a horse worked hard.

14 2009 Montagny Premier Cru, Le Vieux Château, J M Boillot, Burgundy, France, 13% abv

Goedhuis, £16.83

Montagny in the Côte Chalonnaise is another of those areas of Burgundy where no one disputes the quality of the vineyards, but no one has put his or her back into seeing how good the wines could be. Well, Jean-Marc Boillot is a top-class producer from Burgundy's most expensive district, the Côte d'Or, and here he shows just what these fine limestone soils can achieve: a lovely waxy texture, round, rich but savoury cashew nut and oatmeal weight and a palate-bracing apple acidity and keen streak of stony minerality.

15 2011 Malvazija Istarska, Elido Pilato, Lašići, Istria Peninsula, Croatia, 13.5% abv

M&S, £12.49

My top five Chardonnays

- 2011 Chardonnay, De Bortoli, page 20
- 2010 Chablis Premier Cru, Domaine Alain Geoffroy, page 22
- 2010 Mâcon-Loché, Vin de Bourgogne, Domaine Cordier, page 24
- 2009 Montagny Premier Cru, Le Vieux Château, J M Boillot, page 25
- 2010 Chablis, Domaine William Fèvre, page 26

We're going to start seeing a lot more of Croatian Malvazijas from Istria out on the Adriatic Coast. They range from light and fresh to golden and deep, but it's the fresher styles I go for most. This one is supremely scented and adds a surprising plump lushness to the sunny aroma of white spring flowers and seaside rock dust. The plumpness is juicy pears, peaches and a squidge of banana sharpened up by ripe grapefruit zest. In a year's time, the chubbiness will turn to beeswax and the peachy fruit will start to drip syrup.

16 2010 Chablis, Domaine William Fèvre, Burgundy, France, 12.5% abv

Fortnum & Mason, £17.50, The Wine Society, £13.95

For a decade or more William Fèvre has made textbook Chablis, year after year. This producer doesn't try to force a particular house style on the wine; he just interprets the harvest conditions of each vintage as accurately as he can and lets the wine reflect the quality of the grapes in a pure, direct way. The 2010 vintage was a smashing one for Chablis, and the quality shines through here; beautiful dry, honey and oatmeal-biscuit richness, a little hazelnut and quite a lot of piercing lemon acidity wrapped in savoury cream and shot through with clifftop chalk dust.

17 2010 Chardonnay, Shadowfax, Mornington Peninsula, Victoria, Australia, 13% abv

Majestic, £20

Another magnificent example of how the Aussies are fighting back on the Chardie front to prove that their Chardonnays are some of the best in the world. This comes from the very trendy, cool Mornington Peninsula, south of Melbourne, and has quite a bit of peach fruit, but it's bone-dry, not tropical, is finely balanced with a long, lingering acidity and has a nutty depth from oak that almost tastes as if it were polished by hand.

18 2010 Riesling Kugler, Weinrieder, Weinviertel, Niederösterreich, Austria, 13% abv

Waterloo Wine Company, £13.98

A thrilling example of ripe, full, but dry Riesling from top vineyards just to the north of the Danube. Delightfully fleshy fruit: fluffy apples, mellow pears and white peach, but also a darker note of medlars and russet apple skins. Yet the feeling is always crisp. There's a bright, blossomy scent to go with the ripe lemon and strong undertow of rockface mineral dust.

19 2010 Chardonnay, Wild Ferment, Errázuriz, Casablanca Valley, Chile, 13.5% abv

The Co-operative Group, £10.49

An excellent marriage between ebullient Chilean fruit and savoury French Burgundy, greatly enhanced by using wild yeasts from the vineyard. Errázuriz has made this wine for years, and rarely puts the price up as quality stays relentlessly good. It's a waxy, slightly syrupy wine in texture, but very savoury in flavour, with oatmeal, cashew nut and a touch of good sausage meat dominating the flavour and with serious acidity zapping through.

20 2007 Tokaji Furmint, Holdvölgy Meditation, Moonvalley Wines, Tokaj, Hungary, 13% abv

Justerini & Brooks, £22.28

Furmint is the most important grape in Hungary's great sweet wine, Tokaji. But there are lots of grapes left over from that which get made into dry wine, and the flavours are at the very least unusual. Syrupy maturity and fairly high acid gets mixed up with some pretty interesting fruit: pear and apple cores, greengage, stewed green grape skins. There's even a little honey, but it's like the miserly spread on a seaside guesthouse's breakfast toast. And yet that's enough, because the fruit is corseted, uncertain, too. I called this a 'tweedy' white wine. No, I can't now quite think why.

21 2011 Vermentino, Colli di Luni, Cantine Lunae, Liguria, Italy, 12.5% abv

armit, £12.99

Liguria, that tiny precipitous sliver of rock and cliff in the far north-west of Italy, teetering above the Mediterranean, produces some of Italy's most fascinating wines, but in pretty limited quantities, usually just about enough for the thirsty city of Genoa to gorge itself upon. This is an engaging, full-flavoured yet elegant, silk-dress-rustling-in-the-breeze style from the Vermentino grape, Liguria's best. The acidity is refreshing rather than bracing; round peach and greengage fruit is shaded by an insistent, lingering bower scent of lily, musk and perfumed leather. That's the Ligurian genius – the sea fret, the mist, the breeze off the Mediterranean, as well as the warm perfume and cosy scent of steep cliffside vines in nooks and crannies, bathed in sun and shielded from any meaner elements.

WILD FERMENT

Chardonnay
Made from natural yeasts that yield
into depth and complexity vintages

ERRAZURIZ
CHILE

my top 50 white wines

27

22 2011 Pinot Grigio d'Elena, Joseph, Primo Estate, Adelaide, South Australia 12.5% abv

AustralianWineCentre.co.uk, £18
Pinot Grigio on the label usually suggests a fairly light, insubstantial little thing for carefree glugging and tittering conversation. But not when the mighty Joe Grilli gets involved. Joe never skimps on flavour in his wines, and this is really classy stuff that pushes the Pinot Grigio style as far as it can go. Fluffy apple flesh and pale peach, golden-gage plum skins and bright lemon acidity are tinged by country smoke and laid on a yeasty bed of savoury cream.

23 2011 Soave, Pieropan, Veneto, Italy, 12% abv

Bordeaux Index, £10.78,
Liberty Wines, £12.99
Pieropan is probably the main producer trying to revive the quality and renown of Soave after generations of neglect. His pristine wines show that Soave is a super wine style, not just cheap party wine in a litre bottle. This is lovely, restrained wine, with a sense of fresh rain or dew about it, and every nuance is pale: pale wax, pale apple, pale peach, pale soil, pale everything. This will get deeper and riper if you age it for one to five years, but for now, enjoy its reflective, fleeting beauty.

24 2010 Chenin Blanc Reserve, Land of Hope, The Winery of Good Hope, Stellenbosch, South Africa, 13% abv

M&S, £15.99
Tremendous, self-confident Chenin from vineyards fanned by the cold winds of the Cape's False Bay. It's fat and juicy, but balanced, with smoky, dusty honey, beeswax and peach syrup fatness struggling for ascendancy with pear, banana and melon freshness and soft, boiled lemon acidity.

25 2011 Anthìlia, Donnafugata, Sicily, Italy, 12.5% abv

Oddbins, £12
A great example of the bright, perfumed style of white that Sicily, of all places – hot southern Sicily, almost on the coast of Africa – is now producing. Don't ask me how, but these are some of the freshest whites in all of Italy. This is cool, scented and even manages a streak of metallic minerality. There's a shimmering violet scent and zingy yet soft, refreshing

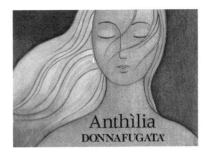

Anthìlia
DONNAFUGATA

peach, pear and ripe grapefruit, all beautifully balanced and demanding to be drunk.

26 2011 Sauvignon Blanc, Iona, Elgin, South Africa, 13.5% abv

Great Western Wine, £12.50
Iona is one of the most southerly Sauvignon Blanc vineyards in South Africa, its vines getting the full blast of the cold, drizzly winds that swirl about the bottom of the continent. These growing conditions produce good, tangy whites, with even a slight spritzy prickle on the tongue, yet the wine is full and ripe, but it's ripe green fruit, not tropical: ripe, green apples and greengages and the soft citrus chewiness of boiled lemons. And all the time, there is a snappy, humming acidity and the chilly, pale minerality of rain-washed stones.

27 2010 Dão Branco, Julia Kemper, Portugal, 13.5% abv

The Oxford Wine Company, £18.75
Dão was Portugal's most famous red wine area for generations, if not centuries – though few bottles appeared that gave one any pleasure when drinking. These were rasping, stone-dry wines. Red Dão is now on a roll, and, clinging to the coat-tails, here comes white Dão: funky, rich, ripe, with a steamy, moist fruit basket of peaches and quince, medlars and baked golden-gage plums drowned in hot custard and topped off with savoury sour cream.

28 2010 Graves Albertine Peyri, Château Beauregard Ducasse, Bordeaux, France, 12.5% abv

Stone, Vine & Sun, £14.95
If I have to keep reminding myself how good barrel-fermented white Graves is, I'm damned certain I'll have to keep reminding you! It's one of France's great white-wine styles that has fallen out of fashion, but all it takes is one mouthful to be persuaded how good it can be. This is bone-dry, but amazingly plump – peach and nectarine and eating apple fruit swirled about with millefeuille

my top 50 white wines

confectioner's cream and icing, nutty, toasty oak and a mouth-warming sense of savoury syrup.

29 2010 Bourgogne Tonnerre Blanc, Domaine de l'Abbaye du Petit Quincy, Dominique Gruhier, Burgundy, France, 12.5% abv

Domaine Direct, £18.50–£16.50

These vineyards just to the east of Chablis, are best known – if they're known at all – for producing a pale, limpid Pinot Noir. But white wine seems more natural in these cool, near-Chablis conditions, and this delightful wine does manage to taste fully ripe but resolutely cool in temperature. It has a gentle, honeyed, honey-bread mellow heart, and the fruit is appley, but these are ripe eating apples, not green cookers. And the acid, which you might expect to be sharp, is hardly noticeable at all.

30 2011 Albariño, Martín Códax, Rías Baixas, Galicia, Spain, 13% abv

Liberty Wines, £11.99, Majestic, £9.99

The Albariños of northwest Spain seem to get better every vintage. Martín Códax is a big operation, and

has often produced pleasant but unmemorable wines in the past. Not any more. This is the real thing, managing to be soft and aromatic, zesty, windswept and minerally all at once. Cool, fluffy, pink apple and white peaches give the wine a soft, waxy heart, but they're the base for a bright, slightly peppery, green-leaf and grapefruit zest tanginess, rounded off with the cold minerality of sea-swept rocks and just a whisper of sweet lemon flower.

31 2010 Chenin Blanc, Unfiltered Terroir Selection, Springfontein Estate, Walker Bay, South Africa, 14% abv

Private Cellar, £13.99

I almost wondered if this were too much of a good thing in its indulgent, syrupy splendour. But when a deeply satisfying, nutty aftertaste is lingering for minutes in your mouth, you sort of think: no, syrupy splendour will do me just fine, because that syrup is packed with peach and pear freshness and isn't actually sweet. The oak adds even more richness: those hazelnuts, as well as fresh toast, a hint of allspice, and – oops – a drizzle of acacia honey.

32 2010 Semillon, Vasse Felix, Margaret River, Western Australia, 13% abv

M&S, £13.99

Margaret River in Western Australia is more famous for its fabulous Bordeaux lookalike reds, yet Semillon is also a Bordeaux grape – but white. This wine easily matches top dry white Bordeaux in quality, but is just a little leaner, drier even. But it's full of flavour: the green-leaf acidity, green-apple flesh, and touch of coffee bean are very like Sauvignon Blanc, but this greenness is wrapped in custard and savoury cream to create a really tasty, ultra-dry white.

33 2010 Riesling, Theodorus, Pfalz, Germany, 12.5% abv

armit, £12.29

The southern Rhine area of Pfalz south-west of Frankfurt is in the vanguard of new-wave winemaking in Germany. It used to have only four or five famous wine villages and the rest were disregarded, unsung and unloved. But now fine wine is turning up all over the region – I had to get my Michelin road map out to find out where Theodorus came from, in the village of Hainfeld nicely tucked up against the forests of the Haardt Mountains. And it's really invigorating stuff – almost tingling on your tongue, properly dry, mixing a good nutty weight with a hint of butter on leather, honey on stones, and a real squirt of lean green apple juice acid.

34 2011 Domaine Coteau de la Biche Vouvray Sec, Domaine Pichot, Loire Valley, France, 12% abv

Goedhuis, £11.92

If you only think of Vouvray as a medium-sweet style of wine and, more often than not, a bit yucky – think again. This one is aggressively dry, pretty acidic, and yet it performs the Vouvray magic of seeming to be fully ripe in its slightly disconcerting, green-dominated way. The baked green apples seem to be drenched in gooseberry syrup but then coated with a savoury cloak somewhere between nuts and cream and a sliver of grilled pork chop.

my top 50 white wines

35 2010 Mâcon-Verzé, Domaine Leflaive, Mâcon-Villages, Burgundy, France, 13% abv
Corney & Barrow, £18.95

Verzé is a lovely village, hidden away in a hillside valley north of Pouilly-Fuissé in the Mâconnais – but I still wouldn't expect to be paying £18.95 for a bottle of its wine unless it was made by the stellar Leflaive family from Puligny-Montrachet. There, Anne-Claude Leflaive makes some of the greatest – and most expensive – of all Burgundies, so perhaps £18.95 for a bottle of Leflaive suddenly sounds more reasonable. And it is rather good stuff: soft yet serious, spicy, gentle, with deep apple and honey richness, tempered by a streak of mineral dust and the pleasing chewiness of ripe apple skins.

36 2008 Gewurztraminer, Zephyr, Glover Family Vineyards, Marlborough, New Zealand, 14% abv
Flagship Wines, £14.49

The generally accepted wisdom is that Gewürztraminer wines don't age. Well, that's probably why no one ever attempts it. Except me.

I've had some beauties at home from under the stairs, and obviously Flagship agrees. This comes from the family vineyards of one of Marlborough's best winemakers and has a lush, languid quality, some not quite dry pear fleshiness, its floral perfume mixed with fresh leather, and fattened up with biscuits crunched into crème fraîche.

37 2010 Falanghina, Via del Campo, Quintodecimo, Campania, Italy, 13.5% abv
Justerini & Brooks, £23.28

I'm not happy about the self-important heavy bottle – that alone probably puts a quid or two on the price – but the liquid inside is seriously good. Falanghina is becoming a fantastically popular grape in the hills inland from Mount Vesuvius, and this shows why. Fascinating wine. Quite fat, or chubby, rather, with a parade of different perfumes: ripe, floral, tropical – the heady aroma of peach orchards and orange groves mingling together with the kind of floral scent of the soap you find in a smart hotel when you get upgraded. A ripeness of sweet lemons, sun-bleached peaches, jasmine and nutmeg and nutty cream. I'm beginning to understand how they get away with the price.

38 2011 Vernaccia di San Gimignano, Principe Strozzi, Tuscany, Italy, 12.5% abv

Laithwaite's, £8.99

A *very* funky Vernaccia. Much of the wine from San Gimignano in Tuscany is made into fairly angular, thin stuff which is gulped down by the thousands of tourists with necks stiff from craning upwards towards San Gimignano's famous towers. Not this one. It positively *wouldn't* refresh you after a hard morning's sightseeing. In fact, if you gulped it back I'd recommend a siesta rather than any more architecture. It's big, ripe, almost heavy, packed with fluffy baked apple flesh, just a whiff of blossom and a serious dollop of yeasty, leesy, funky cream.

39 2011 Burgundy, Grand Vin de Bourgogne, France, 13% abv

Lea & Sandeman, £12.95

This comes from Davayé, a top Mâconnais wine village huddled right up against the gaunt and mighty rocks of Pouilly-Fuissé. The grapes aren't much different from those grown for Pouilly-Fuissé, but you pay a lot less. This is delicious direct Burgundy which you can drink now or age to greater depth over two or three years. It manages to be full and soft, yet keeps a lean acidity, its waxy texture is just dashed with syrup and its creamy, yeasty weight is perfectly balanced with apple fruit like the taste of an unwashed russet picked straight from the tree.

my top 50 white wines

40 2011 Sauvignon Blanc, Cellar Selection, Villa Maria, Marlborough, New Zealand, 13% abv

The Co-operative Group, £10.99

If you pay a little bit more for your Villa Maria Sauvignons, you get a much more exciting wine. Cellar Selection on the label means what it says: loads of wine comes into their cellar, and they cream off some of the best stuff for this label. And you get a real blast of ripe gooseberry and green capsicum that makes you realize why we fell in love with New Zealand Sauvignon in the first place. Add some ripe Bramley cooking apple, some lime-zest sharpness and some slightly funky crème fraîche richness and I say don't change a thing.

41 2010 Sauvignon Blanc, Touraine, Domaine du Chapitre, Loire Valley, France 12.5% abv

Hicks & Don, £9.95

Touraine is making more and more excellent Sauvignon Blanc wines, challenging Sancerre and Pouilly-Fumé for the title of the Loire Valley's best Sauvignon region – and at a lower price. In fact, if you like lots of green flavours, Touraine beats Sancerre

and Pouilly-Fumé, regardless of price. This example is positively intense, managing to be sharp yet rich, a powerful array of green apple, grapefruit, pear pips, blackcurrant leaf and coffee beans washed with honey.

42 2010 Txomín Etxaníz Getaria (Txakolí), Getariako Txakolina, País Vasco, Spain, 11.5% abv

The Oxford Wine Company, £19.99

I had my first taste of Txakolí in a rain-sodden campsite near Bilbao in the Basque country when I was a student. Since there was very little difference between it and cider, I stuck, rather gratefully, to cider. How things have changed. Bilbao now has the Guggenheim Museum and its modern art, Basque cuisine is *über*-cool, and Txakolí is positively revered. I think that's going it a bit – but it's a rare wine – it isn't easy to ripen grapes in Spain's damp north, so I suppose the price is just about bearable for what is a very fresh, tingling style, surprisingly deep, dense even, somehow mixing baked apple flesh and dates with the chewiness of apple peel and the nostril-twitching aroma of lemon zest. Intense, acid, spritzy-fresh and fascinating.

43 2010 Viognier, Ridgeback, Paarl, South Africa. 14% abv

The Real Wine Company, £12.99

This isn't an aromatic Viognier – all brightness of mayflowers and the Mediterranean scents of a bowl of fresh apricots. No, this has been picked very ripe and made in oak barrels and so it's a pretty rich mouthful. It smells of Italian biscotti, toast and roasted hazelnuts and when you taste it, although it is pretty oaky and rich, it all blends in remarkably well and you realize there is good fruit there married with the wood, because you couldn't make a wine this well-balanced without it.

44 2010 Grüner Veltliner Summerer, Langenlois, Weingut Summerer, Kamptal, Niederösterreich, Austria, 12% abv

M&S, £9.99

I was always going to like a bright, fresh, thirst-quenching white made by a guy with a name like Summerer. Grüner Veltliner is an Austrian speciality, and the great swathe of south-facing slopes above the town of Langenlois, just north of the Danube, contain the grape variety's best sites: not too hot or cool, but all the sun

My top five Sauvignon Blancs

- 2010 Sauvignon Blanc, Cape Crest, Te Mata, page 20
- 2010 Sauvignon Blanc, McNaught & Walker, page 22
- 2011 Sauvignon Blanc, Iona, Elgin, page 29
- 2011 Sauvignon Blanc Cellar Selection, Villa Maria, page 34
- 2010 Sauvignon Blanc, Touraine, Domaine du Chapitre, page 34

that you need to produce this fascinating fruit salad of slightly underripe apples, peaches, lemon pith and greengage plums, sprinkled with pepper and mineral dust and yet fattened up with salty, savoury pastry dough. All that flavour and only 12% alcohol.

45 2011 Atlantis White (90% Assyrtiko), Estate Argyros, Santorini, Greece, 13% abv

M&S, £10.49

The EU-protected geographic indication (IGP) for this wine is

my top 50 white wines

Cyclades: those tiny dots of islands that once made up part of the ancient Minoan civilization. Santorini is the main island – what's left of it after a massive volcanic explosion dumped most of its land mass into the Med over 3000 years ago– and quite how vines survive on this windswept, bone-dry island, I don't know. But they do, just, and the 60-year-old vines, hugging the earth in the hope of drinking a little morning and evening dew, produce this remarkable lean yet full white, with dry fluffy apple fruit, a scent of lavender, jasmine and hops, a twist of lemon zest and some funky yeasty texture to stop it being just too lean.

46 2011 Sauvignon Blanc, Sevilen, Florent Dumeau, Aegean Region, Turkey, 12.5% abv
M&S, £9.99

Wow, Turkey is making progress. Even a few years ago, a wine as fresh and zingy as this would have been unthinkable. This comes from the Aegean southwestern part of Turkey, where they've been making a big effort with both vineyards and wineries, and is a delightfully fresh, direct Sauvignon, tingling on the tongue,

leafy, lemony, juicy-green-appley, with a touch of soft cake dough and salty cream to finish it off.

47 2011 Sauvignon Blanc, Coteaux du Giennois, Domaine de Villargeau/Marc Thibault, Loire Valley, France, 13% abv
M&S, £8.99

Perhaps because Sancerre has become so expensive, the lesser-known areas of the Loire Valley have upped their game recently and begun to make delicious Sauvignon Blancs – often better than Sancerre, and at much lower prices. Coteaux du Giennois is a pretty obscure appellation just north of Sancerre, but there's nothing wrong with its vineyards. This wine has an irresistible gentle, fresh texture, touched by summer earth, scented with hop leaf and pears, tasting of soft, green, apple sauce, melons and pears, sharpened by lemon acidity and fattened just a touch with pastry crust.

48 2011 Tămâioasă Româneasca Sec, Prince Stirbey, Dealurile Olteniei, Romania, 13.5% abv

The Wine Society, £9.50

One day Romania will begin to re-claim its historic position as one of Europe's leading wine countries, and it may be through really original wines like this that she'll achieve it. The grape is native to Romania and is worth keeping an eye out for – because this wine is round and plump, mixing rich peach syrup with a little sweet potato (I mean it!), a whiff of half-caught floral scent and the tasty bitterness of orange pith. Well done, Wine Society, for taking a punt on this one.

49 2011 Semeli, Mantinia Nasiakos, Mantinia, Greece, 12% abv

The Wine Society, £10.95

The Moschofilero grape gives this wine a delightful, perfumed character – Greece is full of marvellous grape varieties we rarely see over here. Another true original, a seductive mix of the floral and the citrus. Rose-petal perfume wafts off the glass and makes you expect something soft and lush. You don't get it. You do get very ripe and aromatic grapefruit zest, white melon flesh and the sweet-acid bite of boiled lemons.

50 2010 Bourgogne Chardonnay 'Back to the Roots', Domaine René Lequin-Colin, Burgundy, France, 12.5% abv

Bordeaux Index, £11.28

'Back to the Roots' this label proclaims, and if that means 'back to the vineyard' – a domaine with the vines grown and cared for by a single proprietor, not a great commercial company – then I'm all for it. This domaine is in Santenay, at the southern end of Burgundy's Côte d'Or and I can really taste the Côte d'Or class here: nuts and oatmeal, gentle savoury cream, a lick of acid and the rough kiss of Santenay stones and rock. Restrained stuff, but classy white Burgundy nonetheless.

my top 50 white wines

MY TOP 50 RED WINES

1 2010 Crozes-Hermitage, David Reynaud, Rhône Valley, France, 12.5% abv

Liberty Wines, £18.99

Find me a red wine more lovely, more seductive than this. It's a beautiful, seamless wine made from grapes picked at a mere 12.5% alcohol which makes the efforts of some of its 14% and 15% neighbours look clumsy and laughable. A haunting scent of summer evening jasmine runs right through the wine, mingling thrillingly with the sweet blackberry and mulberry fruit just tickled with the crunchiness of black pepper and celery, yet wrapped in savoury cream and cut through with a gleaming, glinting mineral, like quartz caught in the early morning sun.

2 2005 Viña Alberdi Reserva, La Rioja Alta, Rioja, Spain, 12.5% abv

armit, £15.99

Wines like this are why the Rioja region became famous. Yet these types of wines are under threat from big, raw beasts dark in heart and hue and owing nothing to generations of understated brilliance by guys like these. Its colour is beginning to turn, its smell is that of a beautiful spinster's scent, of nuts and the creamiest of good cream cheese and ripe old fruit tiring of waiting to be plucked for the after-dinner plate. Old strawberries, old red plums, even a richness more like golden-gage plums, but always just beginning to show their age. Yet the balance is perfect: no wasted tannins, and an acidity like a playful and continuous pinprick on your cheek.

3 2007 Barolo Bussia, Giacomo Fenocchio, Piedmont, Italy, 14% abv

armit, £34.99

I know it seems expensive, but, believe me, this is a bit of a bargain for top-quality Barolo, arguably Italy's greatest wine. Deep, strong, true to its purpose.

Your nose bristles with the tannin waiting to pounce, yet it's a tannin that somehow smells like polished pewter. The fruit is dark and almost shrivelled: black cherry, blackberry and strawberry, strewn with mineral shards. And still the tannin is amazingly well behaved, like a crusty Classics teacher sombrely reflecting on a teenage love, a fleeting smile warms his brooding countenance; and for you as the fruit gradually reappears to perk up your spirits and promise you a respectable modicum of indulgence and fun.

4 2010 Syrah, Woodthorpe Vineyard, Te Mata Estate, Hawke's Bay, New Zealand, 13% abv

Berry Bros. & Rudd, Flagship Wines, The Oxford Wine Company, Selfridges, £15.99–£17.95

Hawke's Bay in New Zealand's North Island is rapidly establishing itself as one of great cool-climate sites for the Syrah grape. The Woodthorpe vineyard is actually up a side valley, away from the main action, but the famous Te Mata winery planted some stunning up-river terraces with the objective of making a cheaper line of wines than the mainstream Te Matas, and it has succeeded triumphantly. This has just a suggestion of lily-flower scent, but rather more of the sap of the lily stem, the crunchiness of black pepper and celery just dusted with glittery quartz, then soaked in ripe loganberry and raspberry fruit and the chocolate sweetness of carob.

5 2009 Shiraz, Tim Adams, Clare Valley, South Australia, 14.5% abv

AustralianWineCentre.co.uk, Tesco £12.50

I think Tim Adams' Shiraz has given me more pleasure over the years than almost any other Australian wine. And while similarly fine Aussie reds seem to shoot up in price every time I think of buying a bottle, Tim Adams Shiraz barely seems to keep pace with inflation. This is wonderfully scented wine, almost reeking of blackberry juice, and the scent of black plums with a purple bloom bursting over them, still on the bough, just starting to ooze nectar, and the merest nudge would knock them to the ground and the wasps would swarm. Round, juicy, just a whiff of herbs, a nip of tannin and a splash of dark-chocolate syrup.

7 2007 Nero d'Avola di Sicilia, Santa Cecilia, Planeta, Sicily, Italy, 14% abv

Great Western Wine, £23.50

I've been tasting this vintage for quite a while now, and it just gets better and better. The genius of the Nero d'Avola grape is that it is absurdly delicious when it's literally being squirted out of the vat: fizzing with a fresh, joyous blackberry fruit that you really don't expect in such a hot, sunny place as Sicily, but as it ages, sure, the wine mellows, but the riot of blackberry and blueberry richness is undiminished, a delicate lily scent still flits above the rim of the glass, and you try to tell yourself maturity has made it more serious, but it hasn't.

6 2009 Cabernet/Merlot, Girt by Sea, Voyager Estate, Margaret River, Western Australia, 14% abv

Justerini & Brooks, £17.28

Voyager is a wonderful estate in Western Australia that never loses sight of the fact that red wine is to be drunk joyfully, not merely sipped and spat. This is very ripe – blackcurrants and black Rosa plums pushed to their limits – yet the famous Margaret River freshness holds. There's a little refreshing leafiness and a dusty mist that dries the fruit and keeps the wine supremely appetizing.

8 2010 Pinot Noir, Eradus, Marlborough, New Zealand, 14% abv

Corney & Barrow, £14.95

The vines for this were grown in one of the coolest parts of Marlborough – the Awatere Valley – where the Sauvignons are greener and crunchier, and the Pinot Noirs are a little less lush than most Marlborough Pinots. But that's not a bad thing, because this wine has a mouth-watering scent of red fruit and blackcurrant leaf, and while the acidity is marked, it's a ripe cranberry kind of acid, tossed with rocks and wild, blasted herbs and boiled lemon zest – all teasing the full, soft strawberry fruit but only succeeding in creating a cool, deep, thoughtful Pinot Noir.

9 2010 Shiraz/Viognier, The Lane Vineyard, Adelaide Hills, South Australia, 14% abv

Corney & Barrow, £14.95

This comes from one of the coolest vineyard areas in South Australia, high in the rainy, wooded hills above Adelaide. The Barossa barons probably say you can't ripen Shiraz up there. Well, you can. It just doesn't taste remotely like the Barossa stuff. The wine is wonderfully mellow, a minty perfume followed by ripe Victoria plums and black cherries daring themselves to turn to blackcurrant. The dash of Viognier in the mix brings herbs and peach stones and bright, fresh summer air after a rainstorm.

My top five Shiraz/Syrahs

- 2010 Crozes-Hermitage, David Reynaud, Rhône Valley, page 38
- 2010 Syrah, Te Mata Estate, Woodthorpe Vineyard, page 39
- 2009 Shiraz, Tim Adams, Clare Valley, page 39
- 2010 Syrah, Hervé Souhaut, Vin de Pays de l'Ardèche, Domaine Romaneaux-Desteze, page 42
- 2010 Syrah, Corralillo, Matetic Vineyards, page 42

10 2010 Châteauneuf-du-Pape, Closerie de Vaudieu, Famille Bréchet, Château de Vaudieu, Rhône Valley, France, 14.5% abv

Liberty Wines, £21.99

2010 was a helluva vintage for Châteauneuf-du-Pape, and this is a bit of a beast. Ideally I'd decant it for hours before drinking, or in fact shove it under the stairs for a good five years to let it calm down. But it is the real thing. There are some trendy and absurdly expensive Châteauneufs that are so thick and cloddish they'll never make for a happy mealtime drink.

my top 50 red wines

This one will. It is still tannic and bitter, but it has a beautiful, warm, floral scent, dense, deep loganberry, raspberry and mulberry fruit, crème brûlée richness and delightful refreshing acidity running through the heart of the fruit.

11 2010 Syrah, Vin de Pays de l'Ardèche, Hervé Souhaut, Domaine Romaneaux-Destezet, France, 11.5% abv

Les Caves de Pyrène, £21.99

I like this label. 'Syrah – Hervé Souhaut'. That's all it says. Minimalism. Confidence. Come and try my wine. With the help of my Michelin map, I find that it comes from a tiny village near a steam railway, well to the west of the Rhône Valley, but the flavours would make a Hermitage grower proud. Scented with lilies, a scent that runs right through the lush, juicy, blackberry, pear and peach richness, dusted with ginger and nutmeg, scoured just gently with plum stones and celery, pepper and lily sap. With all that to savour, who needs more on the label?

12 2010 Syrah, Corralillo, Matetic Vineyards, San Antonio Valley, Chile, 14% abv

armit, £14.39

There are some great things going on in the cooler, coastal parts of Chile, and Syrah has found a sensational new home along the Pacific coastline. This wine manages to be almost sticky in its black fruit, yet is bursting with life and vitality. The blackberry and Rosa plum richness is like sauce reduced to jam in a pan, but a savoury peppercorn bite and the bitter-edged brilliance of springtime wood sap hurtle through the heady fruit to prevent it from cloying and congealing. This wine shows the great, cool-climate Syrah paradox: super-ripe fruit versus the roughness of leaves and pepper, wood sap and a brush of coal dust from a collier's apron.

13 2008 Syrah, Steam Wharf Road, Tin Pot Hut, Hawke's Bay, New Zealand, 12.5% abv
Tesco, £14.99

This is a great example of how New Zealand's Hawke's Bay is establishing itself as a top cool-climate red wine area. It started out concentrating on Merlot and Cabernet, but recently it's Syrah that is taking the plaudits. Here's why. The wine's dry, but fantastically full of almost syrupy loganberry and blackberry fruit, but this is challenged by celery salt and white pepper before being pushed aside by chunks of smoky toffee and chocolate, and right then the fruit returns to take back centre stage.

14 2010 Cabernet Sauvignon/Merlot, Moda, Joseph, Primo Estate, McLaren Vale, South Australia, 15% abv
AustralianWineCentre.co.uk, £30

Don't hurry this wine. I've kept the odd bottle of this to see how it ages. Well, it just gets better and better, and I'm not sure any of mine are even ready yet – and we're going back 10 vintages here. This 2010 will probably be the longest-lasting ever because Joe Grilli is using much higher-quality grapes than he used to. He dries these grapes to concentrate their flavours before fermenting them, and the first impression is of a dense, chewy, black wine. But swirl the glass, take your time, and slowly dark, sweet blackcurrant, black cherry and Rosa plum fruit emerges, some mint and eucalyptus scent, some pastry dough and toffee softness, even while a little tongue-tingling sourness pokes its fingers into the wine's ribs. Drink it now if you must, but all of this promise will exhibit a rare brilliance in 10 years' time.

15 2007 Vinho Regional Lisboa Tinto, Quinta de Chocapalha, Castelão, Portugal, 13.5% abv
Corney & Barrow, £11.50

I lose track of the number of times I've said Portugal offers some of Europe's most exciting flavours at prices that just cry out, 'Buy me!' But I'm saying it again. Here's another fascinating red, from the indigenous Castelão

my top 50 red wines

grape – Portugal has dozens of excellent indigenous grapes, too. The flavour starts and finishes with ripe blackberry fruit, but in between there's an explosion of nostril-teasing South Indian black peppercorn, dried herbs like lemon thyme, redcurrant jelly, ripe acidity and grainy tannin that slightly furs your tongue in a refreshing way.

16 2009 Shiraz/Grenache, Wallace, Ben Glaetzer, Barossa Valley, South Australia, 14.5% abv

Great Western Wine, £17.95
One of the most encouraging trends that seems to be emerging from Australia is that the big, overpowering Barossa Shirazes that were beginning to turn me off what had been one of my favourite wine areas are starting to rein in the power and their, frankly, silly levels of ripeness. Hopefully because they realize there's no point in making stuff that people can't drink. I used to find Wallace just too much, so this 2009 is really encouraging: still big and ripe, with a touch of baked fruit about it, but there's good acidity which makes such a difference. There's also sweet black cherry and

blackberry fruit, and the bitter-sweet bite of licorice.

17 2009 Côtes du Rhône-Villages, Plan de Dieu, Domaine de l'Espigouette, Rhône Valley, France, 14.5% abv

Harvey Nichols, £13.50
Big, lush, yet serious southern Rhône red, but that's exactly what you want in a rip-roaring vintage like 2009. A lot of Rhône vineyards got just a bit too baked in 2009, but not these. The wine smells positively bright and breezy, but when you taste it, that ripe strawberry sauce and raspberry jam fruit, warmed by sun-soaked rocks, brushed with sprigs of hillside herbs sweetened with honey and acacia, is actually a really good example of what the Grenache grape in the Rhône loves to do: please the crowds when young, but have the stuffing to age for years if it needs to.

18 2008 Petit Verdot, Monticello, Paul Shaffer, Second Edition, Veritas Vineyard, Virginia, USA, 13% abv

The Oxford Wine Company, £17.99
The US state of Virginia seems to make a point of taking grape varieties

that everyone else finds difficult to grow and turning them into star wines. The white Viognier is the most obvious example, but Petit Verdot – a notoriously late-ripening, tough-skinned, variety from Bordeaux – looks to be a worthy standard-bearer for reds. This has all the deep, black Petit Verdot character, but the fruit is a sweet, rich mix of black plum and blueberry, fattened up with brioche pastry and chocolate and freshened by a nice nip of acidity, along with a dusting of old kitchen spice.

19 2009 Syrah Reserva, Aymura, Geo Wines, Elquí Valley, Chile, 14% abv

M&S, £11.99

These Syrahs from the virtual desert conditions of Elquí, right at the northern tip of Chile's vineyard regions, really are amazing. They're dark and deep, but in perfect balance, unlike many dense New World Shirazes (Shiraz and Syrah are the same grape). This one is amazing, almost shockingly scented for a red wine: a mixture of lilies and a bonfire of branches from a pepper tree. The taste is simply packed with blackberry and loganberry fruit, with a shimmering summer scent almost like warm creosote, a hint of talcum powder and a whole bunch of other dry fruit and mildly peppery herby flavours.

20 2010 Le Clos, Domaine le Clos du Serres, Languedoc, France, 13.5% abv

Oddbins, £11.25

So many of the best vineyards in the South of France are huddled up against the mighty mountain range that becomes the Massif Central. Greater height above sea level and cooling breezes tumbling down from the hills allow for much fresher, more balanced fruit than in wines from the hot flatlands near the Mediterranean. This is an excellent example. Most of the grapes are from the almost-extinct Oeillade variety, helped by Syrah and Grenache, and this mix creates a satisfying, soft, red wine, rich but balanced, laden with loganberry and blackberry fruit, scented with herbs and rock dust and with the gentle chewiness of red cherry skins.

21 2009 Priorat Salmos, Torres, Cataluña, Spain, 15% abv

Slurp.co.uk, £17.70, Waitrose, £16.99
Priorat, named after the region near Barcelona, has become one of Spain's most sought-after wines. Many are insanely expensive, and frankly too dense to enjoy all that much. But Miguel Torres has always managed to mix high quality with affordability and drinkability, and his Priorat demonstrates this.

This has the glyceriney, almost syrupy texture of Priorat, the deep, stewed cherry, date and prune flavours of typical Priorat, but it also has a lick of smooth, rocky minerality, some sweet, bitter licorice and smoky Harrogate toffee and fruit cake soused in brown oloroso Sherry and anise. An intriguing marriage of the wild and the well-brought-up.

22 2006 Tassinaia, Castello del Terriccio, Tuscany, Italy, 14% abv

Lea & Sandeman, £23.95
Top Tuscan reds need a few years to soften and show their true colours. This Tassinaia is now six years old and starting to relish its maturity. It's haughty, austere – the core of the wine is a sturdy stew of black fruit, sun-ripened tomato and black chocolate sucked of all its sweetness. Through all this rumbles a tumbrel of dry stones as scents of wild herbs and cedar rise silently into the air.

23 2011 Cinsault Viejas Tinajas, De Martino, Chile, 13% abv

Les Caves de Pyrène, £11.99, The Wine Society, £8.95
It wasn't many years ago that ancient Cinsault vines like these would have been uprooted if anyone was prepared to pay to do it. Luckily, nobody was, and they survived. In and out of the valleys of the Coastal Mountain range, south of Santiago, people are excitedly discovering more and more old plots of forgotten vines producing small amounts of fantastic grapes. With this wine the De Martino family has really gone back in time and

fermented it in old earthenware jars or *tinajas*. The result is brilliant: a chubby, soft flavour of red cherry sauce, pears and peach flesh, scented with aniseed and rosehip and slapped with the chewy dryness of wood bark, shoe leather and mountain dust.

24 2010 Coteaux du Languedoc, Clos des Mûres, Château Paul Mas, Domaines Paul Mas, Languedoc, France, 14% abv

Old Butcher's Wine Cellar, £12.99
The producers have obviously set out to impress with this wine because there's a lot of toasty oak here. I initially thought it was too much, but then a beautifully intense fruit flavour of blackberry brushed lightly with grilled meat and a little kitchen spice took over, and the oak fell into place. Suddenly it seemed very classy and integrated and the wine itself serious, delicious – and, yes, impressive.

25 2009 Shiraz, Heartland, Ben Glaetzer, Langhorne Creek, Limestone Coast, South Australia, 14.5% abv

Great Western Wine £13.50,
Oddbins, £15

Heartland started out as a fascinating project developing new vineyards in the woody hinterland of South Australia's Limestone Coast. The flavours these grapes produced were awesome, but they couldn't keep up with demand, so began to blend in softer, juicier fruit from Langhorne Creek. So the wines are not now quite so eye-popping, but the remarkable Limestone Coast flavours are still there: eucalyptus, rosemary, lemon verbena acidity, intense blackcurrant – and these are mixed with a black purple scent, black treacle and licorice bittersweet depth from Langhorne Creek. Well worth a try.

26 2009 Blaufränkisch, Triebaumer, Weingut Günter Triebaumer, Burgenland, Austria, 13.5% abv

Nick Dobson Wines, £12.60
I can't resist putting this whacky wine in. The reason I love Austrian reds is that they are so different from the reds of the rest of Europe that we know much better: France, Spain, Italy and so on. Don't expect lush, sun-kissed ripeness; it's a lot cooler up in Austria, and ripeness here is the ripeness of red peppers, red cherries, red plums

and sweet beetroot. The texture can be positively syrupy, the tannin more like the graininess of peach skins, but the red fruit always keeps a super-cool challenging edge to it.

27 2009 Château Reysson, Cru Bourgeois, Haut-Médoc, Bordeaux, France, 14% abv

Oddbins, £15

We must make the best of the 2009 vintage while we can. The weather conditions produced super-ripe flavours in the grapes, which in some places might result in hefty, baked wines, but not in the cool, maritime conditions of Bordeaux. Château Reysson lies just a few kilometres in from the wide Gironde estuary, and the grapes

always relish a little extra sun. This 2009 is positively scented, an aroma of purple plums rising in the glass. The fruit is of ripe blackberries, gently roughened by dry earth but filled out with black chocolate laced with cream. Drink it now or keep it for up to 10 years.

28 2009 Pinot Noir, Domaine Drouhin, Willamette Valley, Oregon, USA, 14% abv

Oddbins, £27

Oregon, on America's northwest shore, is often toasted as a 'new Burgundy'. Well, it took the Burgundians 1,000 years to get things right, and Oregon has a way to go yet, but Véronique Drouhin of the famous Burgundian family has committed herself to producing the best Pinot Noir in Oregon, whether it's Burgundian in style or not. What this does have is fabulous focus. The flavours are quite delicate, but they unerringly hone in on your tongue's sweet spot. This is beautifully scented, with a mellow flavour of red plums and strawberries, juicy and fresh, and just streaked with a little grape-stem sap and herbs. If this is Burgundy in Oregon, I'm all for it.

29 2006 Priorat, Cartoixa, Scala Dei, Cataluña, Spain, 15% abv

Waitrose, £30

The Scala Dei winery was established in the twelfth century, high in the mountains south of Barcelona on dark slate soils. Its wines are world-famous, and many are far more expensive than this, but I love the balance between power and drinkability in this *cuvée*.

It has a brooding, syrupy richness of raisins, dates, sultanas and prunes, and this is fenced in with fairly gritty tannins, but they don't jar bitterly on your tongue, and they let a warm meat-stew savouriness mix with the fruit and mingle with a scent of mountain herbs and old cathedral wooden pews.

30 2010 Pinot Noir, Peregrine, Central Otago, New Zealand, 13.5% abv

Majestic, £20

Each year Central Otago, way in the south of the South Island, tries to claim the crown as New Zealand's finest Pinot Noir producer. It always produces some of New Zealand's best Pinot, yet there are now sufficient numbers of producers in other areas both in the North and South Islands, that it's never a foregone conclusion. But it keeps the southerners trying harder. Peregrine regularly makes one of the top wines, and this has an almost chubby ripeness and density of fruit, but matched by good, almost salty acidity and just enough tannic bite. It's not bitter: more like chewing on scented plum skins as you digest the deep blackberry and strawberry fruit.

31 2010 Fleurie, Clos de la Roilette, Domaine Coudert Père et Fils, Beaujolais, France, 13% abv

Domaine Direct, £15.99-£12.99

Fleurie is supposed to be the most lovely, the most deliciously, scentedly come-hither of all the Beaujolais *crus*. Which is its problem: popularity. The name is so easy to fall for that an awful lot of mediocre wine is pumped out under its beguiling title. But the good stuff does exist, and Domaine Direct is a stickler for importing the real thing and nothing but the real thing. This is sheer delight: a riot of raspberry fruit,

My top five Pinot Noirs

- 2010 Blondie, Wooing Tree, Central Otago, page 24
- 2010 Pinot Noir, Eradus Marlborough, page 40
- 2009 Pinot Noir, Domaine Drouhin, page 48
- 2010 Pinot Noir, Peregrine, page 49
- 2010 Pinot Noir, Tesco Finest, Jenny Dobson, Central Otago, page 56

along with the pips; crème fraîche lushness; and rain-splashed vineyard stones and vine stems. No jam, no make-up, just Fleurie.

32 2009 Syrah, Private Bin, Villa Maria, Hawke's Bay, New Zealand, 13% abv

Majestic, £12.49

New Zealand Syrah is fantastic stuff. There's been too much overripe Syrah turning up from the world's warm vineyards recently, but Hawke's Bay in North Island could hardly be called over-warm. The moderate ripening conditions – along with more bottle maturity than usual; it's a 2009 – allow this Syrah to exhibit a fabulous lily-flower scent,

perhaps even a little sap from the lily stem. There's always a crunchy pepper flavour that is soaked in raspberry sauce and dabbed with the aroma of fresh leather.

33 2009 Cabernet Sauvignon, Peñalolen, Domus Aurea, Maipo Valley, Chile, 14% abv

Majestic, £8.99

The Clos Quebrada de Macul vineyard belonging to the Domus Aurea winery is a wonderful place to visit, hanging high off the mountainside as it does, way above the city of Santiago, still catching the warm evening sun as the crowded capital sinks into shadow. This extra altitude and perfect sun exposure give this Cabernet Sauvignon a lovely pure, blackcurrant fruit. The wine is focused and mouth-watering, with just a touch of smoke, perhaps, drifting up from the houses below, and a rocky, tannic chewiness that seems to blend perfectly with the gentle texture of the fruit.

34 2009 Chianti Classico, Querciabella, Tuscany, Italy, 13.5% abv

armit, £19.99

Chianti isn't the easiest of wine styles to love. I sometimes think the people who go dizzy-eyed over it are often more smitten by the beauty of the Tuscan hills and the charm of the lifestyle rather than the taste of the wine. But this is the kind of stuff that just might get me enthusing more about Chianti. It's perfumed, for a start; it begins with some cherry blossom and the aftertaste is more like pomegranates. In fact pale cherries and pomegranates course through the wine, mingling with a mineral chewiness. It cries out for a *bistecca,* but I could drink this happily while I waited for the grill to warm up.

35 2010 Cabernet Sauvignon, Vin de Pays d'Oc, Domaine de Saissac, Languedoc-Roussillon, France, 13.5% abv
Corney & Barrow, £7.75

This comes from the Minervois area of southern France – usually a bit warm for growing fresh-flavoured Cabernet. Yet they manage it here triumphantly. The wine is deep and ripe, quite dense, and will improve and soften over the next year or so, but the tannic bitterness is easily held in check by the warmth of summer earth and the richness of plums and blackcurrant laced with peach. Big, lush, yet delightfully fresh.

36 2009 Dolcetto d'Alba, Bricco dell'Oriolo, Azelia/Luigi Scavino, Piedmont, Italy, 13% abv
Justerini & Brooks, £9.78

Dolcetto means 'little sweet one' in Italian and I often wonder whether the locals are just having a laugh, since so many examples from this grape are chewy and raw. I still wouldn't say this had the easy 'little sweet one' charm but it's good wine from a respected Barolo producer: quite deep in flavour and slightly chewy, but the chewiness is like plum and cherry skins. There's a little raisin sweetness, and I tell myself I can taste a fleck or two of rock dust from the grape skin's bloom.

2010
Shiraz Durif
Coonawarra
Rutherglen

Both Barrels

37 2010 Shiraz/Durif, Both Barrels, Coonawarra, Rutherglen, Australia, 14.5% abv

Laithwaite's, £9.99

I could just about imagine blending Shiraz and Durif, because they both grow in Australia's warm regions. Well, the Durif here is indeed grown in the hot Rutherglen region of Victoria – famous for liqueur Muscat stickies – but the Shiraz is grown in super-cool Coonawarra in South Australia. It's a totally unexpected yet wildly successful blend: broad and thick-limbed in texture, yet contriving to come up with a magician's brew of blackberry, blueberry and mint, eucalyptus gum, coconut, vanilla and even a scratch or two of lemon zest.

38 2008 Bordeaux, Lea & Sandeman (Carteau-Dabudyk), Bordeaux, France, 13.5% abv

Lea & Sandeman, £9.50

If the old wine-trade adage 'Trust your wine merchant' means anything, it has to apply to the ability to offer tasty, affordable basic Bordeaux: the 'Englishman's claret' of old. Good, trustworthy contacts in the less trendy parts of Bordeaux are absolutely crucial. This comes from the very serious, yet still underrated area of Fronsac, and it immediately exhibits real Fronsac style: dark, ripe, plummy fruit, a little plum-skin chewiness and acidity, and a real sense of the vineyard earth with a seam of iron running through it.

39 2009 Langhe Nebbiolo, Sottimano, Piedmont, Italy, 14.5% abv

Lea & Sandeman, £16.75

Wow: as a winemaker you have to concentrate to get the best out of the Nebbiolo grape, and only the best producers get anywhere near teasing it into creating exciting wine. The Sottimano guys are good. The wine (from young Barbaresco vines) is quite bitter – Nebbiolo always is – but this mixes very well with a dry, black fruit based on the skins (not the flesh) and a perfume, which is partly dusty wax, partly well-worn shoe leather, and partly a curious, tired yet determined, unwilling quality of flowers.

40 2010 Shiraz, EVS, Peter Lehmann, Eden Valley, South Australia, 14.5% abv

Majestic, £12.49

Peter Lehmann is a famous producer of rich, deep, Barossa Valley-grown red wines. But up in the hills of the quaintly and optimistically named Mount Lofty Ranges above Barossa is the Eden Valley: a cooler, higher district best known for its whites. However, they do grow reds, in particular Shiraz, and this is a prime example, with more scent than you'd find in Barossa Valley fruit, the bloom on black plums mingling with the powerful aroma of eucalyptus trees, the sweetness of blackberry fruit and just a touch of lime-juice acidity.

41 2010 Areni Noir, Karasì, Zorah, Rind, Vayotz Dzor, Armenia, 13.5% abv

Liberty Wines, £22.99, Philglas & Swiggot £23.25,

I was initially put off by this wine's big fat bottle, but then I managed to decipher the label and discovered that this was Armenian, from its best wine region, Vayotz Dzor, and made from the indigenous Areni grape – so far as I can tell, unrelated to any other, but possibly really ancient because the first wine grape vines probably developed around here. Also the wine has been aged in earthenware amphorae (*karasì* is the Armenian for 'from amphorae') – that's not so

old-fashioned in places like Armenia – so I couldn't resist the liquid itself. It's only mildly off-beam, only off the lower part of the wall: big and dark, smelling slightly of bark and sap but with rich yet hard-edged black cherry and black plum fruit scratched with acid, trampled with celery and soothed by beeswax.

42 2009 Brouilly, Château du Pavé, Michel Brac de la Perrière, Beaujolais, France, 13% abv

Christopher Piper Wines, £11.17
This really shows the quality but also the warmth of the 2009 vintage. It's remarkably rich for a Beaujolais: very, very ripe, with a sweet core of dates and raisins from the summer heat, yet remains remarkably balanced and refreshing. The richness is well-matched by red cherry freshness, and tasty acidity, as well as a little stony chewiness and a wholehearted sprinkle of kitchen spice.

43 2007 Syrah Reserva, Viña Mayu, Elquí Valley, Chile, 14% abv

Asda, £8.48, Majestic, £7.49
Gosh, these wines from Chile's Elquí Valley are good, and they're sensational value, too. Nowhere else crams so many flavours into the bottle for this amount of money, and wraps them in such a palate-soothing texture. The flavours are also paradoxical, but they blend so well: white chocolate with white pepper, celery with juicy black plums and succulent blackberry, showered with mineral dust from the Atacama Desert.

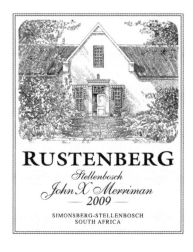

44 2009 John X Merriman, Rustenberg, Stellenbosch, South Africa, 14.5% abv

Lea & Sandeman, £12.50, Majestic, £13.99, SAWinesOnline.co.uk, £12.29

Rustenberg is one of South Africa's most reliable wineries for reds and whites full of substance and flavour. You may need to age the reds, though, to get the best out of them. This is powerful, deep as ink, solid as oak. In fact there's quite a lot of oak richness here, but the big, black fruit is equally rich, if a little chewy just now. If you age it for up to eight years, all the hard edges will drop away and be replaced by sweet fruit and the scent of cedar.

45 2009 Bordeaux Supérieur, Château Brassac, Bordeaux, France, 13.5% abv

The Co-operative Group, £11.99
Really attractive, mouth-watering basic Bordeaux, showing all the class of the super-ripe 2009 vintage as well as the quality of the vineyard. Salleboeuf is not a well-known village, but it does have some good vineyard land, and Brassac sits on a prime chunk. The majority of the grapes are Merlot, which gives soft, dry, red cherry and plum fruit with a buttery, savoury edge, a bright, minerally earthiness and a mellow, glyceriney feeling in your mouth.

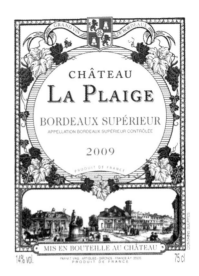

46 2009 Bordeaux Supérieur, Château La Plaige, Bordeaux, France, 14% abv

Stone, Vine & Sun, £8.50
Artigues is not a well-known wine village, but a good wine merchant knows there are good patches of vineyard land in most villages; his job is to find them, and in a fine year like 2009, even the most self-effacing vineyard can excel itself. This is a good example, with surprisingly rich, blackcurrant fruit and a chunky, mouth-filling texture freshened with

green, leafy acidity and softened by earthy cream. If you open this for a few hours before required, or decant it, it will become softer still, and you'll think you're drinking a delightful, traditional St-Émilion – at a great deal less money.

47 2010 Pinot Noir, Tesco Finest, Jenny Dobson, Central Otago, New Zealand, 13.5% abv

Tesco, £10.49

Central Otago is New Zealand's trendiest, coolest (both climate and image) and most expensive vineyard area – way down towards the South Pole – and Pinot Noir is the most expensive red-wine style that New Zealand makes. So it is encouraging that Tesco has managed to keep this price below £11, as well as sourcing a good example with real Central Otago character. This is a juicy red, with deep, slightly stewy loganberry and blueberry fruit and with good cool-climate acidity and the swirl of herbs as well as a trail of smoke and a real sense of the icy glaciers standing guard over the vines.

48 2009 Barossa CSM, Marauding Vintners, Barossa Valley, South Australia, 14.5% abv

Virgin Wines, £11.99

This is a pretty wild mix of grapes. Barossa is famous for Shiraz, and they sometimes mix it with Grenache and Mourvèdre, but this is an unholy trinity of Shiraz with Cabernet Sauvignon and Malbec. Luckily, it's delicious. Ideally open the bottle for an hour or two and the strength of blackcurrant, black treacle and spice will overpower the coconutty oak and add a little mint, lime and carob sweetness to make a lovely, lush blend.

49 2010 Côtes du Rhône-Villages, Château Rochecolombe, Rhône Valley, France, 14.5% abv

Vintage Roots, £11.75

Don't read the chaotic back label – it'll take your thirst away. Stick with the liquid, which is very good and not chaotic at all. This is a powerful, dense, black wine that you could age successfully for up to 10 years, and it does have a black chocolate bitterness, but this is outgunned by a surprisingly scented character, and a sweet but fresh stew of blackberries and black plums with their skins left on.

50 2011 Côtes du Roussillon, Château Saint Nicolas, Roussillon, France, 14% abv

Waitrose, £7.99

Roussillon reds can be just a bit too ripe and baked; the 2010 vintage of this overdid the heat a bit. But when they get it right, the combination of sunshine, wind, and savage, herb-strewn, rocky-hillside conditions can produce really lovely stuff. This red has delicious, deep, dark, sweet blackberry and loganberry fruit, with chewy, 'skinsy' acidity, and a real sense that there's some perfume in the heart of the wine trying to struggle to the surface.

50 wines
for £6-£12

Wine drinkers get hit at least as hard as everyone else in the economic crisis. You might say even harder. The reckoning is that tax on wine will rise by 50 per cent to 60 per cent between 2010 and 2015. Whatever happened to those ill-remembered dreams of The European Single Market, where half our EU partners pay nothing to almost nothing on their bottles of wine while we now pay more than any other EU country? That's 'Single Market' as in where 'there are votes in it'. Clearly there don't seem to be votes in being kind to the wine drinker, even if we are in a majority in the UK. But despite times being tough, an awful lot of us are compensating for the tough times by buying better wines. In the last year, sales of wines over £10 grew by 32 per cent in the UK, and sales of wines costing £7–£8 grew 30 per cent. That's the beating heart of this £6-£12 section. This is where more and more of you are deciding to spend your wine money. And this is where the action truly is. There are 50 fantastic wines in this section, but do check out the Top 100 reds and whites on pages 18-57. Significant numbers of these are under £12, too.

- In this section you will find white wines first, then reds, in descending price order.

WHITE WINES

2011 Albariño, Eiral, Bodegas Pablo Padin, Rías Baixas, Galicia, Spain, 12.5% abv

Wine Rack, £11.99

I'm always encouraged when I pour a glass of Albariño and a spritzy haze develops in the wine that slowly dissipates and leaves a swirl of minute bubbles lying on the surface. I want to feel the freshness of the Atlantic air, the frequency of the squalls, the rain dew left behind. This manages all that beautifully, barely bending its head towards ripeness, but never tasting raw. The apple is lean yet almost fully ripe, but the bitter acid bite of grapefruit pith and lemon zest and the rock dust making your nostrils tingle are the real personality of this wine.

2010 Chardonnay, L'Oeuvre de Perraud, Domaine Perraud, Mâcon-Villages, Burgundy, France, 12.5% abv

Liberty Wines, The Secret Cellar (tel 01892 537981), £11.99

There's been such an improvement over the last few years in the quality of Mâcon-Villages, that affordable high-quality white Burgundy, once a pipe dream, is now increasingly available. Single-domaine wines are popping up all over the place, and here's a beauty, with classic, savoury oatmeal and hazelnut richness and mouth-watering apple and lemon acidity, lightly smeared with honey and sprinkled with rock dust.

2010 Chardonnay/Semillon/Viognier, Winifred, De Grendel, Tygerberg, South Africa, 13.5% abv

Henderson Wines (tel 0131 447 8580), Old Butcher's Wine Cellar, Soho Wine Supply (tel 020 7636 8490), £11.99-£10.99

Quite an ambitious blend of three fairly self-confident grapes. But then, De Grendel makes a pretty confident style of wine; for a start, calling a wine 'Winifred' gives the impression that you hoe your own row. You've got a round, mellow style

here from some barrel-fermentation (nicely done, just fattening up the fruit) and it suits the cashew-nut softness of the Chardonnay, the leafiness (almost blackcurrant leaf) of the Semillon, and the fat-lipped lushness of the Viognier.

• The **De Grendel Merlot** is also a good, rich, fruity example of South African red (£12.50–£11.50).

2010 Garnacha Blancha, La Miranda de Secastilla, Somontano, Aragón, Spain, 14% abv

The Oxford Wine Company, £11.55
This comes from Somontano, a cool area up near the Pyrenees – and you don't really expect to see the warm-climate Garnacha Blancha grape growing there. But the restrained high altitude produces top flavours: rich but dry apple and peach, a texture of wax and syrup and a warmth of biscuit and sun-baked nuts.

2011 Riesling, Seifried Estate, Nelson, New Zealand, 12.5% abv

Flagship Wines, Handford Wines, £10.99
Nelson is next door to the more famous Marlborough region on New Zealand's South Island and has a slightly balmier climate. They claim they have more sun. They do have more rain. And that creates a delightful, fresh yet mellow fruit in the Nelson wines. This Riesling is almost like a ripe German Mosel – it has the honey, the lime marmalade, the lemon blossom, honey and minerals – and yet it doesn't quite have the focus a fine Mosel would have. But that doesn't matter. It isn't a Mosel; it's a lovely, not quite dry Riesling from Nelson.

• And if you fancy something scented with peach blossom and rose petal, dusted with talc yet surprisingly sharpened up by grapefruit and lime zest, then the **Seifried Gewürztraminer** is spot on (The Oxford Wine Company, £10.99).

white *wines* for £6–£12

2009 Verdejo, Finca Montepedroso, Rueda, Castilla y León, Spain, 12.5% abv

James Nicholson, £10.99

Rueda is an unlikely place to produce one of Spain's finest dry whites. It's a broad, open landscape with a relentlessly beating sun, but the Verdejo grape can cope, and has become famous for producing Sauvignon-like wines. This does have leafy greenness and some attractive earthiness, but its real personality is rounder and fuller, even going so far as pineapple chunks, white melon and a nectarine Danish – if such a thing exists.

2011 Grüner Veltliner Classic, Altenriederer, Traisental, Niederösterreich, Austria, 14% abv

Nick Dobson Wines, £10.80

2011 has produced some very exciting Grüner Veltliners: marvellously fresh, marrying ripe fruit and acidity in equal measure. The pleasure starts with a perfume of white flower and pale rock dust. The fruit is ripe green apples – the core as well as the flesh – juicy pears and golden-gage plums and the acidity has that not-quite-sharp quality of boiled lemons with a scratch or two of the lemon zest.

2011 Sauvignon Blanc, Black Label, Yealands Estate, Awatere Valley, Marlborough, New Zealand, 13.5% abv

Great Western Wine, £10.75

Yealands' vineyards are in the Awatere Valley district of Marlborough. It's cooler and windier down there, and the grapes always retain a really snappy, tangy, green quality, but they're not raw. This is an appetizingly ripe wine, but it's a green ripeness, with green apples, green pepper, gooseberries and green-skinned pears, along with scrunched-up blackcurrant leaves and a couple of fresh-roasted coffee beans.

2011 Chardonnay/Viognier, Vignes de Nicole, IGP Pays d'Oc, Château de Conas/Domaines Paul Mas, South of France, 14% abv

Majestic, £9.99

Viognier seems to have found a real vocation as the blending partner for Chardonnay in southern France. Its wines can sometimes be just a bit too lush and apricotty by themselves, but added to Chardonnay, and given a tweak or two of oak ageing, and the combination comes up with this peach-blossom-scented style with waxy apple and smoky peach fruit and round, soothing texture.

• The **Paul Mas Estate Marsanne** is also good (Majestic, £8.99).

2010 Chardonnay Reserve, Jacob's Creek, Adelaide Hills, South Australia, 13.5% abv

Sainsbury's, £9.99

Because Jacob's Creek is such a well-known commercial brand, it's easy to lose sight of the fact that, under the Reserve label the company makes some extremely classy reds and whites, and probably sells them for less than they are worth. This is a beautifully restrained Chardonnay from the damp, cool hills above

Adelaide, more French than Aussie in style, with dry hazelnut and oatmeal cut brightly with lemon acidity and sporting a long, lingering, savoury aftertaste.

2010 Côtes de St-Mont, Le Passé Authentique, Plaimont Producteurs, Southwest France, 13% abv

Waitrose, £9.99

They've got some wild grapes down in France's southwest. This challenging mouthful comes from Gros Manseng, Arufiac and Petit Courbu – *not* grapes I could identify in a blind tasting, because I'm not really sure what they're supposed to taste like. Here they come together in a mighty wodge of high acidity, honeysuckle, ripe crab apples, hillside rubble and an ancient scent of beeswax honey. Nothing modern but well worth a punt.

2011 Sauvignon Blanc, Zoetendal, Elim, South Africa, 13% abv

The Real Wine Company, £9.99
If you want to taste the real potential of South African Sauvignon, you need to head right down to the squally, stormy tip of Africa and the vineyards of Elim. Here you get a blast of greenness from the icy breezes and you can feel the blast of the ocean winds on the grapes as they huddle together for protection. This is as minerally as a Sauvignon can get – windblown dust and wet, blustery rocks – but there's also a vivid, lean yet full flavour of apple peel, green pepper, gooseberry and blackcurrant leaf to give you a real taste of the far south.

2011 Rustenberg SWB, Rustenberg, Stellenbosch, South Africa, 14.5% abv

The Co-operative Group, £9.99
A right old hotchpotch of grapes – Semillon, Viognier, Grenache

and Marsanne – produces a pretty serious mouthful. Loads of peach and apricot and yeasty cream, veering between the apricot jam filling of a baked sponge tart and the creamy fruit of an organic peach yoghurt. It's nutty, too, with a dry, syrupy aftertaste. This will be even better in a year.

2006 Semillon, Sainsbury's Taste the Difference, McWilliam's Wines, Hunter Valley, New South Wales, Australia, 10.5% abv

Sainsbury's, £9.99
Great value for one of Australia's classic whites. Not one of Australia's easiest whites to understand – I'd never accuse Hunter Valley Semillon of that – but this is a seriously good, mature white for less than a tenner. It's a style you may have to get used to: rough, chewy things bundled up with gun metal and wrapped in old leather and buttered toast;

tree bark, apple core and lemon pith trying to come to terms with the butter cream on kids' cakes. But it's worth the effort.

2011 Pinot Grigio, Viña Laguna, Agrolaguna, Istria, Croatia, 13% abv

Lea & Sandeman, £9.95

The Istrians are coming. A couple of years ago you'd hardly have found a single example of the whites from Croatia's Adriatic coast on our shelves. Now these lovely, light, scented, summery whites are starting to arrive, with their soft, mellow character of honeyed fruit: melon, golden cherries and sweet apple, with bright, white-flower perfumes and unobtrusive acidity

and minerality. The Istrians talk of their land as being suffused with 'the lightness of being'. These whites manage to provide real concentration of flavour in harmony with the lightness of being.

2011 Grüner Veltliner, Terraces, Domäne Wachau, Wachau, Niederösterreich, Austria, 13% abv

Waitrose, £9.29

I don't know if you think of stones as 'lickable' on a regular basis, but there is something so stony and yet so disarmingly pleasant to the tongue about this Grüner Veltiner that I'm going to have to repeat myself. It has a flavour like honey spread on smooth, lickable stones. That's not the only taste, though; there's very attractive fluffy apple flesh, chewy apple peel and a softness like bun dough and syrup. Yet it's the stones – and their lickability – that stick with me.

2010 Chardonnay, Limoux, Domaine de l'Aigle, Gérard Bertrand, Languedoc, France, 14% abv

Majestic, £8.99

For a southern French white wine, this is surprisingly restrained and mild-mannered – but that's because the grapes grow in some of the Languedoc's cooler white-wine vineyards, at Limoux, near Carcassonne. Chardonnay likes these relaxed conditions, and produces a gentle white, dry but soft, flecked with spice, splashed with a perfumier's 'outdoors acacia' scent and just lightly touched with indulgent honey and cream.

2011 Sauvignon Blanc, Indo, Anakena, San Antonio Valley, Chile, 13.5% abv

Majestic, Old Butcher's Wine Cellar, £8.99-£7.99

This is the wine for those of you who just fell in love with New Zealand Sauvignon, and wondered why it no longer tastes quite the same. Take heart: it has been reborn on the Pacific Coast of Chile, and here's the proof: all the green flavours you could want – green leaf, green pea, lime zest and gooseberry – plus dust from the valley floor, and a surprising sweet-apple richness. Wherever cool climate vineyards appear in the New World, expect exciting Sauvignon Blanc to follow.

2011 Sauvignon Blanc, La Grande Cuvée, Dourthe, Bordeaux, France, 12% abv

Waitrose, £7.99

Smashing stuff. Bordeaux does snappy, vibrant whites so well when it wants to, I wish more of the big companies would make the effort that Dourthe does. Fistfuls of ripe green fruit – dense green apple, green pepper, gooseberry and greengage with really snappy, appetizing acid. This combines New World panache and French reserve – and the panache wins. It's as good a branded Bordeaux white as I have ever tasted.

• The **Croix des Bouquets Graves** is also a tip-top example of gently oaked Bordeaux white (Waitrose, £10).

2011 Sauvignon Blanc, Le Grand Ballon, Thierry Delaunay, Loire Valley, France, 12% abv

Waitrose, £7.99

The 2011 vintage wasn't the easiest in France, but there are some delightful

Sauvignon Blanc wines turning up on our shelves from the Loire Valley and Bordeaux. This is a classic Loire white, full of fresh green flavours of apple and leaf, nice bracing acidity (but not raw) and the cool, dry texture of river water running over stones.

• Majestic also does a good **Delaunay Sauvignon de Touraine** at £8.99.

2011 Vermentino, IGP Pays d'Oc, Les Vignes de L'Eglise, Languedoc, France, 13% abv
Liberty Wines, £7.99

You're normally knocking back an Italian wine if you see Vermentino on the label, but this grape variety is ideally suited to conditions in the South of France as well. There it makes pretty interesting wine, with a more vibrant freshness than many of the much more usual French varieties. This has a typically lush (for Vermentino) apple-flesh flavour, made more interesting by a dash of pear flesh and strawberry, a spoonful of syrup and a light swish of herbs.

2010 Petit Chablis, Caves des Vignerons, Burgundy, France, 12.5% abv
Asda, £7.27

As global warming conspires to produce ever-riper grapes across Europe, styles that rely on greenness, stoniness, leanness are under threat, and nowhere is this more evident than in Chablis.in northern Burgundy. Which means that the marginal vineyards which traditionally could manage to produce only thin, pallid wines are suddenly finding that the extra heat is allowing them to make lovely, reserved, minerally wines in the classic Chablis vein, just as many of the supposedly better vineyards are struggling to avoid over-ripening their grapes. This Chablis has a really snappy mineral and acid attack, green apples, lemon acid and steel to the fore, but wrapped in savoury cream and mellow honey to produce a delightful true Chablis style.

2011 Vinho Verde, Quinta de Azevedo, Sogrape, Minho, Portugal, 11% abv
Majestic, Oddbins, Stevens Garnier, Waitrose, The Wine Society, £7.25–£6.75
Vinho Verde seems such a perfect wine for the hordes of us who like to drink, like flavour, but want to keep our alcohol intake down. Why aren't there more good examples on the market? Azevedo is the only good one with any kind of wide distribution. So, we'd better praise it. It *is* good. It really reflects the breezy, choppy Atlantic conditions where the grapes grow. It has a slight spritz; it does bite you with lemon pith and green apple core, and it does have a lovely lean, citrus quality with

the cool chill of glistening, squall-drenched rocks splashed with brine. But this wine is hiding a soft heart and even suggests a subtle peach-flesh indulgence as a final fling when you've swallowed and almost moved on.

2011 Sauvignon Blanc/Gros Manseng, Réserve, Les Montgolfiers, Côtes de Gascogne, Thierry Boudinaud, Southwest France, 12% abv
The Co-operative Group, £6.99
This is a great combination: the bright, leafy, juicy Sauvignon Blanc twinned with the denser, more aggressive, chewier Gros Manseng. You get lots of juicy green fruit, some lemon zest and that fresh, springtime green-leaf scent, but the Manseng adds herbs, sharp lemon juice and the chewiness of green apple peel. A lovely style: New World vivacity playing with Old World fruit.

RED WINES

2010 Pinot Noir, McIntyre Lane, Yering Station, Yarra Valley, Victoria, Australia, 13.5% abv

Laithwaite's, £12.49

Chardonnay is making more noise than Pinot Noir in the cool regions around Melbourne, but places like Yarra Valley were first lauded because they just might have given the Aussies the chance to do something they passionately craved: make decent Pinot Noir. Well, this is more than decent. It has a lovely mellow texture, is restrained yet tasty, with smooth strawberry mixed with syrup of slightly sour cherries. Ripe apples help with the acidity and gentle spice holds it in check. They do try to make Pinot in a Burgundian style. This is it.

2010 Chénas, Domaine de la Croix Barraud, Beaujolais, France, 13% abv

Nick Dobson Wines, £12

Chénas is traditionally the toughest of the top Beaujolais wines, the one you need to age, often more in hope than certainty that the wine will soften. It's the leanest, least Beaujolais-like of Beaujolais. Well, these guys clearly

forgot to make this tough and unfriendly because it's a delight: amazingly rich and juicy for a Chénas, with deep, ripe, red plum fruit jousting with strawberries and pepper and rock dust, uncertain as to which will offer the mineral tang... so they both do.

2010 Chianti Colli Senesi, Salcheto, Tuscany, Italy, 13.5% abv

Selfridges, £11.99

Selfridges has come out with some very cool, ink-drawn labels – quite right, too. They've got a very cool wine department, and this is a really good, traditional Chianti fronted by a portrait of a dude with long hair, designer stubble and statement glasses. The lovely thing about the wine is that it is such a

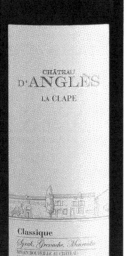

straight and true interpretation of Chianti, not mucked about with or internationalized. That means it is no juicy-lucy red; you get the stubble, not the make-up. It feels grippy and 'skinsy', and the fruit is made up of grudgingly, uncertainly ripe red cherries and plums. The scent is the savoury aroma of lovage, and there's a splash of something so brilliantly malevolent that you can't fully relax with it until they've plonked down a great slab of grilled Valdichiana steak in front of you – and then, it's red-wine heaven.

2008 La Clape Classique, Coteaux du Languedoc, Château d'Anglès, Languedoc, France, 14% abv
Wine Rack, £11.99
La Clape is a proud outcrop of limestone rock rearing up from the hot Mediterranean flatlands near Narbonne, and it produces some of the South's best grapes. The freshness of the fruit is what's so exciting, along with the almost chewy minerality and the surge of hillside herbs. There's a torrent of stewed mulberry, red plum and cherry fruit that has a definite rock and bitter herb-sap twist, but that is easily outweighed by the glorious infusion of bayleaf and rosemary.

2011 Malbec Clásico, Altos las Hormigas, Mendoza, Argentina, 14% abv
Liberty Wines, £11.99
Altos las Hormigas is a very interesting Argentine operation, which takes an Italian rather than New World approach to its wine, and manages to create some of Argentina's lushest Malbecs without the fruit tasting baked or over-ripe. This is helped by a classically Italian hint of sweet-sour in the wine which really rachets up the drinkability-ometer, adding the sweet plum and

damson fruit, the attractively stewy texture and the mingled aftertaste of spice and savoury syrup.

2008 Rioja Crianza, Paco García, Rioja, Spain, 13.5% abv

James Nicholson, £11.25

So calming, so soothing, so mellow… just what I want Rioja to be. There are some wines I buy with a sense of nervous anticipation: what kind of crazy flavours are going to leap out? But when I broach my favourite Riojas, I do so with a knowing smile playing on my lips. The soft strawberry fruit, the mild, creamy texture, the friendly, barely rough kiss of vineyard earth and a polite suggestion of chewy peach skins… these are what I want. And these are what I find.

2010 Côtes du Rhône-Villages, Domaine de Cristia, Rhône Valley, France, 14% abv

Big Red Wine Company, £11

Domaine de Christia is a top estate based in the Châteauneuf-du-Pape village of Courthezon. This wine lacks the concentration – and the exalted price – of a Châteauneuf, but makes up for it with heady scent and bright, ripe fruit. It smells appetizingly of jasmine and lily stems allied with some sap and stemmy greenness, and the perfume runs through the taste, too, with fresh, ripe red fruit unconcerned by the ripe, chewy tannins or even the undertow of bright, clear-eyed stones.

2010 Malbec Reserva, Viñalba, Mendoza, Argentina, 14.5% abv

Majestic, £10.99

Viñalba comes from a French-owned outfit in one of the best parts of Mendoza high in the Andes foothills, and the European approach of relative restraint faced with the bulging, sugar-stuffed Malbec grapes works really well. You can taste the joyous juiciness of the fruit, not just the sun beating down on the vine. But the sun is there in a rich, chubby way as the scented damson and blackberry fruit works out (successfully) how to marry itself with the dates, the milk chocolate fruit 'n' nut bar and the cakey softness of Victoria sponge.

2010 Pinot Noir, Ona Single-Vineyard, Anakena, Leyda Valley, Chile, 13.5% abv

Oddbins £9.99,
Old Butcher's Wine Cellar, £10.99

Anakena is a really imaginative, go-getting winery which has released a series of top-quality single-vineyard reds and whites at very keen prices. Leyda is proving itself to be a fantastic, cool-climate area for reds and whites. This Pinot is soft and waxy, its texture like leather polished with glycerine. A little blossom scent perches lightly on gentle red plum and cherry fruit wrapped in soft, savoury cream.

• Other excellent single vineyards include **Murta Syrah** and **Lilen Viognier** (both Majestic, £9.99).

2010 Douro Red, Quinta do Crasto, Portugal, 13.5% abv

Great Western Wine, £10.95
Quinta do Crasto not only has some of the most breathtaking views in the beautiful Douro Valley, but it has mastered the art of making red Douro table wine a simple thing of beauty, while many of its neighbours continue to overcomplicate and over-oak the stuff. This is an utter delight: scented with jasmine, bulging with ripe black plums, mulberry and blueberry fruit with the merest tug of chewy tannin, and as you swallow, back comes the jasmine.

• **Sainsbury's Taste the Difference Douro** (£8.99) is also good.

2010 Syrah, Charles Smith, Columbia Valley, Washington State, USA, 13.5% abv

Laithwaite's, £9.99
Washington isn't known for easy-drinking reds, and it's not known for bargains, but here you get both. I say 'easy-drinking', but that doesn't mean it isn't a serious Washington red. It's just that it's got all the concentrated fruit so many others promise, yet it isn't fuddled or muddled by too much alcohol and oak and messing about. Concentrated strawberry and blackberry fruit is cut through with quite insistent acid – as though you'd splashed a drop of good vinegar into a cauldron of fruit sauce. It's got all the weight and body you need to be taken seriously, but it's also damned drinkable.

red wines for £6–£12

72

2010 Malbec/Tempranillo, Finca Sophia, Bodegas O Fournier, Mendoza, Argentina, 14% abv
M&S, £9.99

Malbec is a grape that is rarely bested when blended with something else; its rich blast of succulent fruit usually carries off any partners in its fulsome wake. But these Tempranillo grapes come from old plantations cosseted by the winery's owner, and they put up a fight. The deep-purple, plummy Malbec fruit is stood up to by the chewy, savoury yet syrupy, red Tempranillo, the smell is more savoury than floral, the tannin grainy and mouth-watering. Plum against strawberry, syrup against herbs and tannin? That old vine Tempranillo just comes out on top.

• The **Finca Sophia Sauvignon Blanc** (M&S, £9.99) is also well worth a look.

2011 Grenache, Greg Clack, Haselgrove Wines, McLaren Vale, South Australia, 14.5% abv
M&S, £9.99

Grenache is the sex-on-wheels artist among red grapes. Sure, it can do the serious stuff – Spain's Priorat and France's Châteauneuf-du-Pape are pretty serious – but that's not where Grenache's heart lies. Happy juice: that's the cry that goes up when a glass of Grenache is poured. A burst of strawberry fruit, as rich and fresh as a strawberry coulis scratched with lemon zest. Sprinkle on some peppercorns and thyme, and... well, that's it. I said it wasn't complicated.

2009 Kalecik Karasi, Vinkara, Anatolia, Turkey, 13.5% abv
The Wine Society, £9.50

I made my first wine trip to Turkey a couple of years ago, and the difference between old style and new style is as stark as in any wine country. The 2009 vintage is 'new style' and allows the indigenous Kalecik Karasi grape's charm and mellow personality to shine as it has never done before. Stewed red cherries, raspberries, and redcurrant juice coil together with glyceriney fudge and fruit syrup. Many

of the new Turkey's best reds are haughty and challenging wines. This delicious Kalecik Karasi shows her gentler side.

2009 Petite Sirah, DB Reserve, De Bortoli, Southeastern Australia, 13.5% abv

Sainsbury's, £9.49

Petite Sirah has a reputation for being a bit of a beast, but there are one or two corners of the world (literally just one or two) where the beast becomes a scented beauty. Paso Robles in California is one place, and the parched hinterland of New South Wales' Riverina is another. This is still big, dark wine, but it has lost its brutal tannic attack and has replaced it with lush, mouth-filling blackcurrant fruit, bittersweet licorice, and mint toffee.

2010 Dão, Giesta, Quinta da Giesta, Portugal, 13% abv

Laithwaite's, £8.99

Dão reds are usually a bit of a challenge. That shouldn't be a surprise; they've been challenging the taste buds for hundreds of years with their dark, forbidding, bone-dry styles. But at last there's new red blood rushing through their veins. They haven't forgotten the stones and the craggy slopes, but they've finally discovered a vestige of fruit and scent. This is beautifully ripe, full of blackberry and blueberry fruit, but that has to cope with this red's savoury scent, the bloody perfume of the butcher's slab and a tumble of hillside stones. Very serious, but beautiful in an almost solemn way.

2011 Rioja Joven, Single Vineyard, 100% Garnacha, Averys Project Winemaker/ Bodegas Medievo, Rioja, Spain, 14% abv

Averys Wine Merchants, £8.99

Most Rioja is a blend based on the Tempranillo grape, and most Rioja prides itself on time spent maturing in oak barrels. This Rioja is neither. It's made from 100 per cent Garnacha grapes, and that word *joven* on the label shows that it hasn't had any oak ageing at all. The result is tremendous. It's a riot of every sort of strawberry – from just picked berries to summer hols strawberry ice cream on a stick to my mum's last summer's jam being spread thick and lumpy on

melting buttered toast. Add a swirl of herbs and this gives you an entirely new outlook on Rioja.

2010 Carmenère, Averys Project Winemaker/Viña Casa Silva, Colchagua Valley, Chile, 14% abv

Averys Wine Merchants, £7.99

Averys has been running a thing called Project Winemaker: taking a fresh look at some of wine's better-known styles and reinterpreting them. The results are really good, and here's a prime example. Colchagua is famous for Carmenère, but I find many examples a bit soapy and sunburned. Not this one. It has a pervasive dusty, floral scent and fabulously fat, juicy fruit, as though you'd swirled up black cherries and blackcurrants with slices of cling peach. And then in piles the genius of Carmenère. Its savoury side is part vegetal, part meat pie, and all whacked with soy sauce, coffee and peppercorns.

2011 Le XV du Président, Vin de Pays des Côtes Catalanes, Mark Hoddy, Roussillon, France, 15% abv

Laithwaite's, £7.99

The Président's XV sounds more like a rugby invitational team, but that may be closer to the mark than you think: there's some very serious rugby played down in this corner of France. And I bet drinking a few jugs of this would add a bit of muscle to the boys. It's made from 100-year-old Grenache vines grown in the excellent village of Maury: very juicy blackcurrant jam and plum-syrup fruit, appetizing acidity and chewiness keeping the flavour fresh, and a rich, lingering aftertaste of Christmas cake, molasses and raisins.

2011 Malbec Reserve, Finca Flichman, Mendoza, Argentina, 14% abv

Stevens Garnier, Waitrose, £8.99
Finca Flichman is owned by a big Portuguese company called Sogrape, and there are definite similarities here with good Portuguese Douro red. The bright, optimistic jasmine scent with round black-plum fruit is Douro-like, but it also resembles drinkable young Malbec at its best. Add to that some quality milk chocolate, a flash of minerals, a touch of traditional Malbec fish-oil leatheriness and you get good, modern Malbec, the best yet from Flichman and its Portuguese bosses.

2011 Toro Vino Tinto Joven, El Pícaro, Matsu, Toro, Castilla y León, Spain, 14.5% abv

Majestic, £7.99
This has such a cool label. El Pícaro sort of means 'the son' and here he is, in grainy sepia splendour, gazing out at you from under his flat cap. Matsu also makes 'Father' and 'Grandfather' Toros, but I like this one best. It's the youngest, although the vines are 90 years old, and it has only spent six weeks ageing in wood. It gives you all the Toro power you could want without the strong tannin that can make Toro such hard work. It's ripe and deep, dense almost with inky concentration but with sweet, stewed raspberry fruit and the shimmering fumes of the hot, Toro landscape running through the wine.

2009 Teroldego, Tesco Finest, Vigneti delle Dolomiti, Trento, Italy, 12.5% abv
Tesco, £7.99

Teroldego makes utterly delightful picnic red wherever you plant it – I've just had some lovely stuff from Brazil – but Italy's Trentino region is its heartland, and this example doesn't let us down. It has a really smashing dark raspberry and loganberry fruit rubbed with peach skins. A little dusty cream teams up with lean, lithe, stony tannin to create a full-flavoured but breezy red.

2010 Ventoux, Rhône Selection, Étienne Gonnet, Rhône Valley, France, 14% abv
Adnams, £7.99

Ventoux used to make fairly light, sort of semi-Rhône reds. That was then. The soils and conditions are excellent and finally being exploited to make serious reds. My initial impression with this was that perhaps it was too serious. At first sip it's dark and solid and fairly tannic. But the bristly tannin is big and proper – rugged, not rough – and it does peel off in the mouth to reveal a much warmer core of rich strawberry and black cherry simmered briefly with a posy of hillside herbs.

2011 Côte Roannaise, Les Vieilles Vignes, Domaine Robert Sérol et Fils, Loire Valley, France, 12% abv
The Wine Society, £7.95
Good old Wine Society. This is a really rare French wine, but it is an absolute beaut. It's a sort of *über*-Beaujolais – using the same Gamay grape, but from vineyards further to the west, actually on the upper reaches of the Loire. It's rough-and-ready stuff, but a complete delight. There's a bright, chewy turbulence of peach skin and pear skin, strawberry and stones. It's sappy and tasty yet lean, and the stones rub off any self-indulgence that might be clinging to your tongue.

2011 Carignan, Vieilles Vignes, Vin de Pays de l'Hérault, Maison de La Paix, Languedoc, France, 13% abv
Jascots (tel 020 8965 2000), £7.90
I can't believe that the Carignan is still a despised grape variety in France's far south, but how else can I explain the fabulous quality of this wine and its massively affordable price? Well, let's take advantage and lap up this heady mixture of blossom, lush, ripe, red fruit and quarry dust. The strawberry and cranberry get mixed in with peach and pear skin, and the blossom becomes tangled up with those Chelsea-bun kind of cakes, with little lumps of crystallized ginger on the top.

2011 Cuvée des Galets, Côtes du Rhône, Les Vignerons d'Estézargues, Rhône Valley, France, 14.5% abv
Stone, Vine & Sun, £7.75
Galets are the round, flat stones that famously abound in the vineyards of Châteauneuf-du-Pape in the hot southern Rhône Valley. This wine's vineyards are close by – but on the opposite side of the mighty river Rhône, and the warm stones don't quite bake the grapes as they often do in Châteauneuf-du-Pape. You do get a flicker of hot Rhône dust, but this is far more boisterous wine, the strawberry, raspberry and cranberry flavours are as fresh as fruit straight off the bush,

and the texture is so crisp and crunchy it could be a white – but it's gloriously, juicily red.

2010 Corbières, Cave de Castelmaure, Embres et Castelmaure, Languedoc, France, 13.5% abv

Morrisons, £6.95

It warms my heart when I see a big high street player go to exactly the producer I'd have chosen for its in-house wines. The Cave de Castelmaure is a smashing, modern, flavour-focused co-op in Corbières and was one of the first in the whole of France to embrace the New Age of fruit and balance – and earns itself an ocean of satisfied customers. And they haven't missed a beat with this wine. This is lush, mouthfilling stuff, boasting a little jasmine scent and a lot more thyme, and bayleaves so fresh they could be plucked right off the bush. And that's on top of a dark, juicy, blackberry fruit that seems to enjoy the hurly-burly addition of rock dust and grainy tannin.

red wines for £6–£12

around £6

Inflation didn't start to drop in the UK quite fast enough. The inflation-plus-two-per-cent escalator that the Chancellor continues to employ on excise duty kicked in remorselessly once again in 2012, and along with the various other tax rises, and worldwide problems with costs of production, this £6 barrier has looked pretty wobbly this year. Remember, it's only a couple of years ago that this section was concentrating on wines for £4.99. These – those that are left – have now been consigned to the 'Cheap and Cheerful' section on page 92, and several of my favourites this year have been nearer £6.50 than £6. But the majority of wines listed in this section are still below £6 – enough, I hope, to give a good, broad choice to those of you who really don't want to break that £6 barrier.

• In this section you will find white wines first, then reds, in descending price order.

WHITE WINES

2011 Chardonnay, Mâcon-Villages, Cave de Lugny, Burgundy, France 13% abv

Asda, £7.14

A very pleasant, dry Chardonnay from the village of Lugny, which has been well-known for decades without exactly becoming famous. We should be grateful; it keeps the price down. This is very direct; you could almost call it simple, but I prefer 'uncomplicated'; appley fruit rolled in honey, with just a dash of lemony acid.

2011 Chardonnay, Le Manoir du Baron, Vin de Pays d'Oc, Foncalieu/Domaine de Corneille, Languedoc, France, 13.5% abv

Asda, £7.14

It's easy to over-ripen Chardonnay down near the Mediterranean coast in the South of France. Luckily, 2011 was hardly a sunseeker's dream (it was basically on the cool side), but that means the grapes came into the winery much fresher, and the wine is lighter and fresher. This is soft, with gentle apple fruit and a soothing texture from time spent on its yeast lees in the vat.

2011 Sauvignon Blanc, Cowrie Bay, Marlborough, New Zealand, 12.5% abv

Waitrose, £6.99

Classy stuff. Marlborough Sauvignon with this tangy attack would usually cost at least a couple of quid more. They've sourced a lot of the fruit from the ultra-cool Awatere Valley, a sub-region of Marlborough, and that provides a zingy, green pepper, green apple, green leaf crunchiness that has you salivating for more.

2011 The Society's Chilean Chardonnay, Marcelo Papa & Ignacio Recabarren, Limarí Valley, Chile, 14% abv

The Wine Society, £6.50

The Society's Chilean Chardonnay used to be a kind of high-quality bolt-hole for those who wanted their Chardies big and rich and tropical. Well, the twenty-first century has arrived. The grapes are now sourced from Limarí, possibly

Chile's best Chardonnay region; the winemakers are two of Chile's best, and the wine is still full of pineapple chunks, peach, melon and pear – in fact, bursting at the seams, almost – but somehow they've eased back on the throttle.

2010 Garganega, Saveroni, Cantina di Valpantena, Veneto, Italy, 13% abv
Oddbins, £6.50
Garganega is an excellent grape, not as well known as it ought to be because most of it is shovelled into the bland white sea that is called Soave. Here, under its own flag, the wine is bright and scented, with ripe pear and apple fruit dabbed with spice and wearing a light, breezy, blossom perfume.

2011 Falanghina, Rocca Vecchia, Puglia, Italy, 12.5% abv
The Co-operative Group, £6.49
This white wine comes from Puglia, in Italy's far south – that's in the 'heel'. It's blindingly hot down there and you don't expect to be able to grow white grapes with freshness and aroma – but the Falanghina grape, one of southern Italy's best, can cope with heat, and this has a lovely scent of pears and peach

blossom laid over bright acidity and some soft, southern earth.

2010 Sauvignon Blanc, Rueda, Sitios de Bodega (Richard Sanz), Castilla y León, Spain, 12.5% abv
The Co-operative Group, £6.49
Passion fruit and ripe grapefruit zest are both flavours that many winemakers worldwide try to create in their Sauvignon Blancs. The trouble is, if you're not really good the whole shebang can end up smelling slightly of stale sweat. But these guys know what they're doing, and this is very zesty, grapefruity stuff with a lick of passion fruit – and I promise you no underarm.

2010 Pé Branco, Herdade do Esporão, Alentejo, Portugal, 12.5% abv
Christopher Piper Wines, £6.35
This has a fantastically verbose front label – I can't understand a word of it. But the wine? That I can understand. This is a really original, multi-grape offering from the Portuguese hinterland, and it has loads of fruit: juicy apples and pears, peach and a blob of banana, along with some yeasty richness, and a delightfully come-hither freshness.

2011 Viña Sol, Torres, Cataluña, Spain, 11.5% abv
Asda, £6.29

I don't want to wreck the rest of the wine trade's profit margins, but if you're buying either of these excellent Torres brands (the Viña Sol red or white), you should head for Asda who sell it at a very competitive price. The white Viña Sol is a great thirst quencher and is as good as it has ever been: appley, lemony, tangy and fresh.

2011 Chat-en-Oeuf Blanc, Vin de Pays d'Oc, Boutinot, Languedoc, France, 12.5% abv
Waitrose, £5.99

With a name like this (a pun on the well-known Rhône wine, Châteauneuf-du-Pape), you either like it or you don't. But the wine stands confidently on its own two feet. When the South of France uses its own grapes – Grenache, Marsanne and Roussanne here – rather than relying on international stars like Sauvignon Blanc and Chardonnay, the results are delightful. This is full of pear and apple fruit dashed with spice and it has a pale but lingering summer blossom scent.

2011 Pinot Grigio, Mátra Mountain, Hungary, 12% abv
Waitrose, £5.99

This is turning into an annual plea: give Hungary a chance. The vineyards are excellent, the winemaking is good – and at least some of the grape varieties are familiar. Pinot Grigio often stands for a pretty pallid brew, but not in Hungary. Here it's a lovely, gentle, fruity style, all fluffy apples and pear flesh, lightly smeared with honey and flecked with fresh countryside dust.

2011 Verdejo, Rueda, Casa del Monte, Castilla y León, Spain, 13% abv
Old Chapel Cellars, £5.99

The Rueda region is now well known for its fresh whites and the main grape used is the local Verdejo. It's become famous because it's like Sauvignon Blanc – but not quite. This has got good grapefruit zest

and acidity but also has a fullness more like pineapples and a pleasant drying sensation of sunbleached stones.

2011 Sauvignon Blanc, Sacred Hill, Marlborough, New Zealand, 13% abv

Asda, £5.98

I always approach cheap Marlborough Sauvignon Blanc with a certain amount of trepidation. A couple of years ago there was some awful stuff plaguing our market. But this year there's some pretty decent, bright stuff – and this, despite being a touch syrupy, has lots of the green apple, green pepper and gooseberry flavour that first turned us on to Kiwi Sauvignon.

2011 Côtes de Gascogne, Harmonie de Gascogne, Domaine de Pellehaut, Southwest France, 11.5% abv

Booths, £5.89

A really powerful, interesting Gascon wine,

with extra flavours coming from a mêlée of five different grapes, rather than the usual Colombard or Ugni Blanc. So you get quite a blast of passion fruit, some thyme and sage herb scent, snappy lemon juice and zest – a big mouthful for the price.

2011 Muscadet de Sèvre-et-Maine, Champteloup, Loire Valley, France, 12% abv

Waitrose, £5.69

I'm beginning to think that it's time for a bit of a Muscadet revival. I don't always want the blast of a Sauvignon or the weight of a Chardonnay in my white wines. What about a gentle, mellow, bone-dry white, just slightly creamy in texture with a mild melon and apple fruit and an unthreatening price tag? Our parents' generation used to drink Muscadet like water. Well, a lot of it tasted like water. It's much better now.

2011 Catarratto, Casa Lella, Araldica Vini Piemontesi, Sicily, Italy, 13% abv

Asda, £5.68

Increasingly Sicily is becoming the go-to place for value-for-money whites and reds in Italy, as well as producing some stellar stuff further up the price scale. Catarratto isn't Sicily's most scented grape variety, but it gives a delightful mellow wine, soft yet fresh and just flecked with a little spice.

• The **Casa Lella Nero d'Avola** (red) is also pretty good at £4.48.

2011 Cortese Piemonte, Araldica Vini Piemontesi, Piedmont, Italy, 11.5% abv

The Wine Society, £5.50

The Cortese grape used to make very sharp, spiky whites as an antidote to Piedmont's big, bruising reds from Nebbiolo such as Barolo and Barbaresco. Now, it's still sharp, but it isn't spiky anymore, the lemon is milder, the stones smoother, and while the apple core and lemon pith are still bitter, the bitterness fades rather than clings to your teeth.

RED WINES

2011 Pinot Noir, Nostros Reserva, Viña Indomita, Casablanca Valley, Chile, 13% abv

The Wright Wine Company, £6.55

Chile's Pinot Noir sometimes err a little on the syrupy side, and this one does just that – but it's pretty tasty syrup, and well enough balanced with a mildly bracing acidity to make a good, affordable Pinot Noir mouthful – and there aren't many of those. That syrup is a juicy mix of red plums and strawberries, even pears, just tinged with smoke. Pretty nice.

2011 Negroamaro, Feudi di San Marzano, Puglia, Italy, 13.5% abv

M&S, £6.49

Negroamaro means the 'black bitter' grape, and if you grew it in cool conditions, that's exactly how it would taste. But way down in Italy's 'heel', the sun bakes the vines, and although there's a wood-bark bitterness in the wine, it's welcome to counteract the rich, stewy, plum jam fruit and the peppery allspice scent.

around £6 – red wines

2010 Zinfandel, Bear Creek, Lodi, California, 14.5% abv

Morrisons, £6.49

Don't go for overpriced then deep-discounted big-brand Zinfandel; go for the real thing under a non-glitzy label. Lodi is a Californian region making a reputation for itself through fair pricing and soft, juicy, balanced flavours. This is a really pleasant Zin, with sweetish black-plum fruit mingling amiably with raisin and date and a little West Coast summer earth.

2011 Coteaux des Baronnies, Cuvée Traditionelle, Cellier des Dauphins, Rhône Valley, France, 13% abv

Waitrose, £6.29

The Celliers des Dauphins, which make this wine, is a big operation that seems to have taken fire this year with its budget offerings. This wine is relatively light, but that doesn't matter, because it offers really focused raspberry fruit, refreshing acidity and a light slap of herbs.

2011 Cabernet Sauvignon, 35° South, Viña San Pedro, Molina, Chile, 13.5% abv

Sainsbury's, £5.99

Chile is a much easier country than, say, Australia or California, to get good quality wine at £5.99. But the temptation for big brands to dilute their quality remains strong, so it's encouraging that 35° South has come up with a soft wine that still boasts lots of dark, red-plum fruit and pleasant weight in the mouth without any hard edges.

2011 Shiraz/Cabernet Sauvignon, Cape Quarter, Fairtrade, Overhex, Western Cape, South Africa, 13.5% abv
M&S, £5.99
Fairtrade does a lot of important work in the wine regions of South Africa, and is a key factor in improving the lives of the rural poor. Even so, the wine still has to be good – and this one is. Full and round with ripe mulberry and red-plum fruit fattened up with marshmallow and just slightly roughened with smoky earth.

2011 Claret Reserve, Bordeaux, France, 12.5% abv
Waitrose, £5.99
This is pretty young for a Bordeaux red. The secret lies in it being 100% Merlot: a much softer-centred grape than Cabernet. It's full of rough-cut, chunky red fruit, ripe and quite

powerful even, with just enough tannic nip and a winsome scent to balance the clean, chewy earth.

2006 Rioja Reserva, Baron Amarillo, Rioja, Spain, 13.5% abv
Aldi, £5.99
It's good to know that we can still get affordable, mature Rioja. Before the New World wines came along, this type of wine, with its mellow, thoughtful, unhurried flavours, kept us all from giving up drink because of thin, unripe flavours offered to us by our dear neighbour France. It plays a lesser role now, but it's still a pleasure to find its old strawberry and dried-cherry fruit, its touch of savoury cream and hint of oak-barrel texture that doesn't shout at you.

2011 Montepulciano d'Abruzzo, Umani Ronchi, Abruzzo, Italy, 12.5% abv
Waitrose, £5.99
Montepulciano is a tremendous grape, full of plummy depth, but since it is mostly grown in some of Italy's more rustic wine areas, too often the flavours are rustic, too. But this one captures all the dark plum core of flavour but balances it with nice bright

acid which allows the fruit to be juicy and mouth-watering even as the wine itself is pretty solid.

2011 Shiraz/Trincadeira, Tagus Creek, Falua Sociedade de Vinhos, Alentejo, Portugal, 13.5% abv
Asda, £5.98
We need more of this type of red from Portugal. They can ripen both famous varieties like Shiraz and their numerous local varieties like Trincadeira, and with a twist or two of New World winemaking you get all the richness of ripe, red fruit in a really juicy style and just enough acidity and bite to keep it serious. Well, semi...

2011 Beaujolais-Villages, Asda Extra Special, Pasquier Desvignes, France, 12.5% abv
Asda, £5.97
There's some nice Beaujolais around at the moment. The challenge is to get more of us to drink it. Bright, breezy, fruity red, no oak, only 12.5 per cent alcohol, under £6..., that shouldn't be a difficult sell. So come on: this is a juicy mix of strawberry and apples, slightly bruised peaches and banana starting to go black – great with strawberries and cream. Try it!

2011 Vin de Pays d'Oc Rouge, Domaine Laborie, France, 12.5% abv
The Wine Society, £5.50
Good, chunky red that manages to exude a rich, warm, stewy style yet balance it with bright, juicy, crisp, red fruit. There's lots of fruit here, it's dark and rich at its core, but it's the lively, ripe cranberry and red cherry that finally win.

2010 Garnacha Tinto, Cruz de Piedra, Calatayud, Aragón, Spain, 14% abv
The Wine Society, £5.50
Calatayud is of the hidden gems of Spain: full of gnarled old vines giving small crops of intensely tasty fruit. But few people know it so the price stays low. This is simply as rich and ripe a strawberry-flavoured red as you could crave, almost syrupy, but kept appetizing by a sappy green streak and just enough tannin to nip your gums.

2010 Sangre de Toro, Torres, Cataluña, Spain, 13.5% abv
Asda, £5.13
As with the white Torres Viña Sol (see page 84) the red Sangre de Toro is cheaper at Asda than elsewhere. This Sangre de Toro gets better each vintage: cake spice, rich cherry/plum fruit and a nip of tannin.

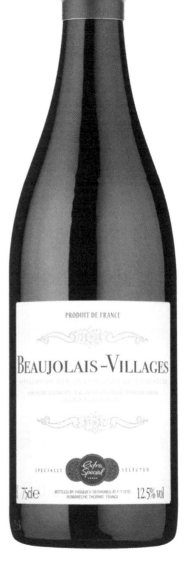

*cheap &
cheerful*

I don't know how they still do it. I'm not sure I want to know how some of our retailers still manage to squeeze a few bottles of reasonably decent grog onto our shelves at under £4. Frankly, few of the wines under £4 are worth wasting time on if you actually prefer your wine to taste of something you're happy putting in your mouth – but there are a couple, so I list them. Last year's four quid is more like this year's £4.50, with relentless price rises from tax, currency and inflation all eating away at any possible profit for producer or retailer. So I've allowed our cheap-and-cheerful ceiling to drift up to nearer five quid – hoping that you'd prefer to pay a few pence more for something half decent. If it's just price that concerns you, well, you don't need advice from me.

- In this section you will find white wines first, then reds, in descending price order.

WHITE WINES

NV Simply Pinot Grigio, Delle Venezie IGT, Cavit, Trento, Italy, 12% abv
Tesco, £4.99

Pinot Grigio has become the byword for amiable, inoffensive and vaguely classy – as against, say, Liebfraumilch – easygoing white. It's also usually at least 50p more than it should be. But this is a pleasant, mild, not-quite-dry white, soft and simple apple fruit, a hint of pear, a dash of lemon... Pretty good.

2011 Chardonnay, Henri de Lorgère, Mâcon-Villages, Burgundy, France, 13% abv
Aldi, £4.99

Not bad, this. It's a Mâcon, from Burgundy in France, and they've had the courage to put Chardonnay – the grape variety – on the label. That sounds an obvious thing to do, you know, being helpful, that sort of thing, but it's surprisingly rare in Burgundy, where they grow loads of Chardonnay. A little white melon, a little honey, a touch of earth and a dash of lemon... Nice.

2011 Chilean Chardonnay, Valle Central, Chile, 13% abv
Morrisons, £4.99

Chilean Chardonnay is famously full of flavour, and some of us may find it just too fruity. But for those who don't, this has got a big, rich, traditional feel to it based on pineapple chunks, boiled sweets, honey and apple syrup with just enough acid to keep it fairly fresh.

2011 Chardonnay/Chenin Blanc, Rincon del Sol, Santa Ana, Argentina, 12.5% abv
M&S, £4.99

This is a pretty sensible combination for a warm place like Mendoza, in Argentina, because Chardonnay gets ripe pretty quickly there while Chenin hangs on to its fresh acidity

much longer. This is nice and fruity, not quite dry, but with good apple fruit and even a little apple-pip chewiness, and a hint of the warm earth.

NV Italian Vino da Tavola Bianco, MGM Mondo del Vino, Italy, 13% abv
M&S, £4.99
Imaginative blend from Sicily in the south, Romagna in the middle, and Piedmont in the north of Italy. The result is a very pleasant, clean, fresh apply wine with mild, lemon-zest acidity. Good fruit for a basic white.

2011 Marsanne, IGP Pays d'Oc, Foncalieu/ Domaine de Corneille, Languedoc-Roussillon, France, 13% abv
Asda, £4

This is quite a full, dry white wine, with just a whiff of honeysuckle, and honey-scented dust. Honey is what the Marsanne grape is all about, so that's about right.

• Asda **Chardonnay** (£4.07) is nice, too.

RED WINES

2011 Gamay, Vin de Pays de l'Ardèche, Cave de Saint-Désirat, Rhône Valley, France, 12% abv
M&S, £4.99
Delightful stuff. This comes from a really good cooperative in the northern Rhône Valley that makes the very classy (and much more expensive) St-Joseph. I suspect this is what the winemakers drink on their picnics; it's so fresh, with barely ripe, crunchy mulberries and rose hips, crumbled green leaves, and earth and dust touched by hillside dew.

NV Sainsbury's House Beaujolais, France, 12% abv
Sainsbury's, £4.79
There's quite a bit of decent low-priced Beaujolais around at the moment, trying to lure us back to a wine we used to love as Beaujolais Nouveau, then discarded in contempt

N DE PAYS DE L'ARDECHE
GAMAY

MIS EN BOUTEILLE À LA PROPRIÉTÉ
PAR CAVE DE SAINT-DESIRAT À F-07360 - FRANCE
POUR MARKS & SPENCER PLC. PO BOX 3339, CHESTER, CH99 9QS, UK
PRODUCT OF FRANCE

– as Beaujolais Nouveau again. Well, this is pretty nice all-year-round Beaujolais: quite fresh, some peach and strawberry and apple fruit and a stony undertow.

2011 Cuvée Chasseur, Vin de France, Les Producteurs Réunis, 12% abv
Waitrose, £4.69
A tip-top basic red, year in, year out. This even has the audacity to sport a bit of floral scent – at the price of £4.69! – to go with its juicy, black-cherry and black-plum fruit, its nip of appley acidity and chewy texture.

NV Sainsbury's House Pinot Noir, Cramele Recas, Romania, 13% abv
Sainsbury's, £4.49
Romania was known for its funky but tasty (and cheap) Pinot Noirs in Communist times. Well, the vines are still there, and the wine is no beauty, but it is full of baked-jam fruit and a fairly rich, glyceriney texture.

2011 El Guia Tinto, Bodegas Borsao, Utiel-Requena, Valencia, Spain, 12% abv
Waitrose, £3.99
A Garnacha red from the very dependable Borsao company.

Full, juicy, round chubby and warm with strawberry and red plum fruit and a slight savoury seasoning.

2011 Pinotage, Origin Wines, Western Cape, South Africa, 14% abv
Asda, £4.17
A challenging mix of mulberries, marshmallows and kindling smoke. Unfamiliar flavours? Yes, indeed. But that's what Pinotage is supposed to taste like – and this is a good, juicy example at a very fair price.

2011 Côtes du Rhône, Cellier des Dauphins, Rhône Valley, France, 14% abv
Asda, £3.67
I was so taken with this that I had to check with the Asda head buyer. 'Is that really the price?' I asked her. 'Can you really guarantee the quality all year long?' She says yes. So here it is: a smashing, fresh, juicy, warm and dusty southern Rhône red with a really good splash of strawberry jam fruit and no hard edges.
• **Tesco's Simply Côtes du Rhône** is pretty similar at £3.65.

Wine's taxing times

- I was talking to a French wine importer as he gloomily surveyed our continuing economic crisis and the latest Budget tax increases. He reckoned that for a supermarket to be able to sell a wine profitably for £5, the producer would end up being paid not much more than €0.60 – that's about 50p a bottle. With excise duty at £1.90 a bottle (and inexorably rising with every Budget) and VAT at 20% (there's also customs duty to add if you're a non-EU producer like Australia), the government is taking an ever-bigger chunk out of our £5 bottle. But shipping costs, distribution, glass bottles, corks and labels all cost, and inflation of several of these is well above the headline rate. Add a profit margin which most high-street and supermarket groups demand be at least 30% and maybe 40% – and that 50p value for the juice in your £5 bottle becomes distressingly understandable. So think: if you bought a £7 bottle, VAT and profit margin would rise a bit, but the other costs wouldn't. If you only get 50p's worth of wine in a £5 bottle, you can get more like £2 worth of wine in a £7 bottle. It still sounds pretty pathetic, but it's a hell of an improvement.

rosé wines

Our love affair with rosé is changing – and for the better. It may have started with a deluge of rather sweet and gooey pink concoctions from California, and they're still over here and none too dear. But the rest of the rosé world is becoming drier, and paler. So pale that you sometimes have to hold the glass near a light bulb to make sure that you're not drinking a faintly blushing white. This move has been led by the French, and above all, the rosés from Provence: the Côte d'Azur, the Monaco Grand Prix, the beaches and babes and drop-dead yachts the size of Berkshire... *that* world. For a long time I've pooh-poohed this world and its pricey pinks, but dammit, the quality is getting so good that I'm having to admit they're increasingly worth the money. And when I see the Spanish, and then, the New World tyros like the Chileans and Aussies going drier and paler... well. This trend could become unstoppable, so let's follow it.

• The wines in this section are listed in descending price order.

2011 MiP – Made in Provence, Domaine Sainte Lucie, Michel Fabre, Côtes de Provence, France, 12.5% abv

Lea & Sandeman, £10.95

This is just one of numerous good Provence rosés on the market at the moment, but it is particularly good. The 2011 wines have more fruit and flavour than usual, and this is matched by a freshness of ripe grapefruit that is quite unexpected in the mellow, inoffensive world of Provençal pink. But that's quickly softened out by banana lushness and a mouth-wateringly juicy, eating-apple aftertaste that lingers just long enough.

2011 Côtes de Provence, Sainte Victoire, Famille Negrel, Provence, France, 13% abv

Majestic, £9.99

Majestic is making a big effort with rosé at the movement – this is only one of several good ones in stock from Provence. But it's a beautiful, water-pale little number, with that telltale extra flavour from the 2011 vintage: juicy apple flesh and pear fruit, wild rose-hip scent and a dusting of icing sugar.

• Other good Majestic rosés from southern France include **Château Pigoudet La Chapelle Rosé Coteaux d'Aix en Provence** (£9.99), and **Château Barthès Rosé Bandol**, (£11.99).

NV Rioja Rosado, Muga, Rioja, Spain, 13.5% abv

Waitrose, £9.49

Rioja is so famous for red wines that we forget how good its *rosados* are. (You could say the same about its underrated whites.) But if you want gentle, elegant, almost scented wines with an appetizing, savoury edge, Rioja is hard to beat. Muga is a particular favourite, partly because the pale-pink wine is fermented for three-and-a-half weeks in old wooden vats. That would give the wine its full, round texture, but the apple fruit, the oak and blossom scent and refreshing acidity – like the merest scraping of lemon zest into the glass – is down to the quality of the single-vineyard grapes.

• Majestic does the 2011 for £9.99.

2011 Mirabeau, Côtes de Provence, Provence, France, 12.5% abv
Waitrose, £8.99

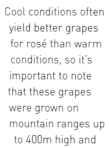

Cool conditions often yield better grapes for rosé than warm conditions, so it's important to note that these grapes were grown on mountain ranges up to 400m high and mostly facing north, away from the fiery Provençal sun. Add to that the fact that they were harvested in the chill of night, and the wine should be pretty fresh. It is. It has that delightful mellowness of Provençal fruit, but also the surprisingly full flavour of soft pear and banana and crisp eating apples (English, of course) that the 2011 vintage brings.

2011 Cuvée Fanny, IGP Cévennes, Domaine Puech-Berthier (Thierry Coulomb), Languedoc, France, 12.5% abv
Fingal-Rock, £7.50
I tried to find out exactly where this estate was, and then realized that, with Fingal Rock as the importer, I'd probably never have heard of its area anyway. Fingal Rock is a dab hand at tracking down the wines the rest of us simply cannot find, even with our trusty Michelin road map. So I leave it to them and they come up with stuff like this 100% Cinsault (that's pretty rare): pale, but very lively, with good apple flesh and pink cherry enlivened by really zippy apple peel and lemon-zest bite.

2011 Les Estivales, Les Vignobles Foncalieu/Domaine de Corneille, Languedoc, France, 13.5% abv
Asda, £7.14
This is verging on the full side for a southern French rosé, but they've done it well, and the result is a very gluggable fresh, juicy style with a bit more flavour than you'd expect. The

rosé wines

101

strawberry taste is pretty ripe and the apple flesh is crisp and crunchy with a refreshing acidity teasing your taste buds and keeping the full flavours in check.

• Asda also does a pretty good soft, dry Spanish rosé for the same price (£5.98) called **Bodegas Borsao Gran Vega Privado Rosé**.

2011 Nero d'Avola Rosato, Il Papavero, MGM Mondo del Vino, Sicily, Italy, 13% abv

Laithwaite's, £6.99

You just can't keep Nero d'Avola down. It's such a smashing grape, with so much exuberant personality and flavour, that it's physically incapable of making a pale,

mild pink. So, accept it for what it is, and settle into a delightfully fresh wine, but one with an almost waxy texture, washing over strawberry and juicy apple flesh, and then cut through with bracing apple-peel acidity.

2011 Garnacha Rosé, Tesco Finest, Bodegas Príncipe De Viana, Navarra, Spain, 12.5% abv

Tesco, £6.99

While most of the rest of Spain is concentrating on drier, paler styles, good old Tesco sticks to its guns and produces a big, juicy, not-quite-dry crowd-pleaser that may be a bit much at room temperature, but will be absolutely fine after a few hours in the chiller. It is a bit syrupy, but there's a big wodge of fat strawberry fruit and wobbly pear flesh rolling about at its heart, so drink it with goose pimples straight from the fridge.

2011 Carmenère/Syrah, Viña Mayu, Elquí Valley, Chile, 14% abv

Asda, £6.48

Some of you may hanker for a rather fuller-flavoured pink. Well, here it is, from the semi-desert wilds of northern Chile. Despite being fairly full-bodied, it keeps a welcome freshness along with piles of flavour. Carménère and Syrah are both pretty tasty grapes more used to making dark-red wines, but here they combine to create quite a rich pink colour, loganberry and apple fruit with a squeeze of lemon acidity and a whiff of drifting smoke. Very Chilean.

2011 Cabernet Rosé, Nagyréde Estate, Mátra, Hungary, 12% abv
Booths, £5.79

Delicious, juicy pink that really tastes of the Cabernet grape. Most rosés spend so little time in contact with the skins – which bear most of a grape variety's character – that they display no discernible characteristics from the type of grape. But this is quite full, very slightly earthy with a definite blackcurrant-leaf freshness rather like a lean, young red Bordeaux. And this is softened by attractive apple-flesh fruit into a very tasty glass of pink.

NV Grenache Rosé, Vin de Pays des Coteaux de l'Ardèche, Luc Talleron, France, 13.5% abv
Sainsbury's, £4.49

Good budget pink from an undervalued but reliable area west of the Rhône

Valley. Pleasant, strawberryish, quite full for a French pink and not quite dry. Chill it right down for a very pleasant drink.

2011 Rosé, Toro Loco, Utiel-Requena, Valencia, Spain, 12% abv
Aldi, £3.59

Don't expect subtlety at this price: the wine tastes as though it has barely finished fermenting, but it has a fair whack of strawberry fruit and some crisp, juicy apples that taste as though they were hurled rather than daintily placed in the picker's basket. But, hey: serve it ice-cold and you've saved enough money to have another waiting in the chiller.

- Waitrose does a similar Utiel-Requena wine called **El Guia**. **Rosado** (£3.99).

keeping it light

We're becoming increasingly disenchanted with high-alcohol wines.
So, increasingly, I'm checking the alcohol content of the wines
I recommend. Here are my suggestions for drinks with fab flavours
that won't leave you fuzzy-headed the next morning.

More and more wines seem to be hitting our shores at 14.5%, 15% – even 15.5%.
That's fine if the alcohol is balanced by ripe fruit and good acidity – but don't
think of these wines as a jolly beverage to knock back with your lamb chops:
you'll be asleep or sozzled before you've got the meat off the barbie.

Now, some wines have traditionally been high in alcohol, and wear their
strength well, but there are far too many wines that – less than a decade ago
– used to perform at 11.5–12.5% alcohol and which are now adding at least
a degree – and often more – to their strength, seemingly in an effort to ape
the ripe round flavours of the New World. Thank goodness there are still a
significant number showing more restraint.

At 12.5% there are lots of wines, particularly from cooler parts of France –
most Beaujolais is 12–12.5% – northern Italy, where the most famous examples
would be the Veneto reds Valpolicella and Bardolino and the white Soave, and
from numerous parts of Eastern Europe, particularly Hungary.

But we've set the bar at 12%. This cuts out a lot of red wines; the slightly tart,
refreshing white styles that sit easily at 12% can develop better flavour at a lower
strength than most reds can. This exercise reminded us that Germany is full
of fantastic Riesling wines as low as 7.5%. Muscadet is usually only 12%. Many
supermarket house reds and whites are 11.5–12%. Western Australian whites
are often 12%. And Champagne, along with most other sparkling wines, is often
only 12%. Hallelujah.

- VdP = Vin de Pays

White wine

- 2011 Airén/Sauvignon Blanc, Gran López, La Mancha, Spain, £4.99, Waitrose, 11.5%
- 2011 Albariño, Eiral, Rías Baixas, Galicia, Spain, £11.99, Wine Rack, 12%
- 2011 Albariño,Viña Taboexa, Rías Baixas, Galicia, Spain, £9.99, Waitrose, 12%
- 2011 Bacchus, Chapel Down, Kent, England, £10.99, Waitrose, 12%
- 2011 Blanc de Morgex et de la Salle, Vini Estremi, Valle d'Aosta, Italy, £14.95, Les Caves de Pyrène, 12%
- 2010 Bourgogne Chardonnay, Vieilles Vignes, Nicolas Potel, Burgundy, France, £11.99, Majestic, 12%
- 2011 Chardonnay/Sauvignon Blanc, Domaine de la Fruitière, Loire Valley, France, £7.99, Waitrose, 12%
- 2011 Chenin Blanc/Pinot Grigio/Királyleányka, Eva's Vineyard, Hilltop Estate, Észak-Dunántul Region, Hungary, £3.99, Waitrose, 11.5%
- 2012 Colombard, La Biondina, Primo Estate, Adelaide, South Australia, £9.99, AustralianWineCentre.co.uk, 12%
- 2010 Colombard/Gros Manseng, Côtes de Gascogne, Vignobles des Aubas, £6.99, Majestic, 12%
- 2011 Cortese Piemonte, Araldica Vini Piemontesi, Piedmont, Italy, £5.50, The Wine Society, 11.5% abv (page 86)
- 2011 Cortese Piemonte, Italy, £5.99, M&S, 11.5%
- 2011 Côtes de Gascogne, Charte d'Assemblage Blanc, Southwest France, £7.99, Waitrose, 12%
- 2011 Côtes de Gascogne, Harmonie de Gascogne, Domaine de Pellehaut, Southwest France, £5.89, Booths, 11.5% abv (page 85)
- 2011 Côtes de Gascogne, Les Quatre Cépages, Domaine de Pajot, France, £7.25, Vintage Roots, 11.8%
- 2011 Sauvignon Blanc/Gros Manseng Réserve, Les Montgolfiers, Côtes de Gascogne, Thierry Boudinaud, Southwest France, £6.99, The Co-operative Group, 12% abv (page 68)
- 2010 Côtes-du-Roussillon Blanc, Palais des Anciens, Vignerons Catalans, Languedoc-Roussillon, France, £7.99, Tesco, 12%
- 2011 Côte Roannaise, Les Vieilles Vignes, Domaine Robert Sérol et Fils, Loire Valley, France, £7.95, The Wine Society, 12% abv (page 78)
- 2011 Cuvée Pêcheur, Vin de France, £4.69, Waitrose, 11.5%
- 2011 Cuvée de Richard Blanc, Comté Tolosan, Southwest France, £5.29, Majestic, 11.5%
- 2011 Domaine Coteau de la Biche Vouvray Sec, Domaine Pichot, Loire Valley, France, £11.92, Goedhuis, 12% abv, (page 31)
- 2011 VdP du Gers, Lesc Blanc, Producteurs Plaimont, Southwest France, £7.49, Les Caves de Pyrène, 11%
- 2011 VdP du Gers, Pujalet, Southwest France, £4.99, Waitrose, 11.5%
- 2009 Gringet, Vin de Savoie, Le Feu, Domaine Belluard, France, £24.49, Les Caves de Pyrène, 12%
- 2011 Grüner Veltliner, Federspiel, Weissenkirchen, Domäne Wachau, Wachau, Austria, £9.99, Majestic, 12%
- 2011 Grüner Veltliner (Höpler), Tesco Finest, Austria, £6.99, Tesco, 12%
- 2010 Grüner Veltliner Summerer, Langenlois, Weingut Summerer, Kamptal, Niederösterreich, Austria, £9.99, M&S, 12% abv (page 35)
- 2011 Grüner Veltliner, Terraces, Domäne Wachau, Wachau, Austria, £9.29, Waitrose, 12%
- 2010 Iglesia Vella, Domaine du Roc des Anges, Languedoc-Roussillon, France, £36.99, Les Caves de Pyrène, 12%
- 2011 Muscadet Côtes de Grandlieu *sur lie*, Fief Guérin, Loire Valley, France, £7.49, Waitrose, 12%
- 2011 Muscadet de Sèvre-et-Maine, Champteloup, Loire Valley, France, £5.69, Waitrose, 12% (page 86)

- 2011 Muscadet Sèvre-et-Maine *sur lie*, Sainsbury's Taste the Difference, Loire Valley, France, £6.49, Sainsbury's, 12%
- 2010 Muscadet Sèvre-et-Maine *sur lie*, Vieilles Vignes, Clos des Allées, Pierre Luneau-Papin, Loire Valley, France, £10.49, Les Caves de Pyrène, 12%
- 2011 Ortega/Reichensteiner/Chardonnay English White, Tesco Finest, Denbies, England, £8.99, Tesco, 12%
- 2010 Petit Chablis, Domaine d'Elise, Burgundy, France, £11.25, Stone, Vine & Sun, 12%
- 2010/11 Petit Chablis, Domaine Gérard Tremblay, Burgundy, France, £13.49, Les Caves de Pyrène, 12%
- 2010 Pinot Blanc, Stopham Estate, West Sussex, England, £14.99–£14.50, Liberty Wines, Vinoteca 10.5% abv (page 23)
- 2011 Pinot Grigio, Mátra Mountain, Hungary, £5.99, Waitrose, 12% (page 84)
- 2011 Riesling, Tim Adams, Clare Valley, South Australia, £10.49, AustralianWineCentre.co.uk, Tesco, 11.5%
- 2008 Riesling, Bishops Head, Waipara Valley, New Zealand, £12.99, Private Cellar, 12%
- 2009 Riesling, Select, Framingham, Marlborough, New Zealand, £16.49, Les Caves de Pyrène, 8.5%
- 2010 Riesling, Main Divide, Pegasus Bay, Waipara, New Zealand, £12.49, Majestic, 12%
- 2011 Riesling, Dr Wagner, Mosel, Germany, £8.99, Waitrose, 8%
- 2011 Riesling Kabinett, Ayler Kupp, Weingut Weber, Mosel, Germany, £8.99, Majestic, 8%
- 2010/11 Riesling Kabinett, Oberhäuser Leistenberg, Dönnhoff, Nahe, Germany, £21.49, Les Caves de Pyrène, 8.5%/10%
- 2010 Riesling Kabinett, Piesporter Goldtröpfchen, Hain, Mosel, Germany, £12.30, Tanners, 8%
- 2009 Riesling Kabinett Trocken, Prinz von Hessen, Rheingau, Germany, £10.99, Majestic, 11.5%
- 2011 Riesling Kabinett, Ürziger Würzgarten, Dr Loosen, Mosel, Germany, c.£15.99, Waitrose, 7.5%
- 2011 Rioja Blanco, Valdepomares, Rioja, Spain, £6.99, M&S, 12%
- 2011 Sauvignon Blanc, Bella, Invivo, Marlborough, New Zealand, £14.50, Harvey Nichols, 9%
- 2011 Sauvignon Blanc, Champteloup, Touraine, Loire Valley, France, £7.79, Waitrose, 12%
- 2011 Sauvignon Blanc, La Grande Cuvée, Dourthe, Bordeaux, France, £7.99, Waitrose, 12% (page 66)
- 2011 Sauvignon Blanc, Le Grand Ballon, Thierry Delaunay, Loire Valley, France, £7.99, Waitrose, 12% (page 66)
- 2011 Sauvignon Blanc, La Grille, Touraine, Loire Valley, France, £7.49, Majestic, 12%
- 2011 Sauvignon Blanc, Les Rafelières, VdP du Val de Loire, Sauvion, France, £7.99, Private Cellar, 12%
- 2010 Savagnin, Springhill, Irvine, Eden Valley, South Australia, £14.25, Vin du Van, 12%
- 2011 Semeli Mantinia Nasiakos, Mantinia, Greece, £10.95, The Wine Society, 12% (page 37)
- 2011 Semillon, Denman Vineyard, Tesco Finest, Hunter Valley, New South Wales, Australia, £9.99, Tesco, 11%
- 2005 Semillon, Margaret, Peter Lehmann, Barossa, South Australia, £14.25, Vin du Van, 11.5% abv (page 21)
- 2006 Semillon, Sainsbury's Taste the Difference, McWilliam's Wines, Hunter Valley, New South Wales, Australia, £9.99, Sainsbury's, 10.5% (page 64)
- 2005 Semillon, Mount Pleasant Elizabeth, Hunter Valley, New South Wales, Australia, £9.29, Tesco, 12%
- NV Simply Pinot Grigio, Delle Venezie IGT, Cavit, Trento, Italy, £4.99, Tesco, 12% (page 94)
- 2011 Soave Classico (Equipe), Veneto, Italy, £4.59, Tesco, 12%
- 2011 Soave, Pieropan, Soave, Veneto, Italy, £12.99–£10.78, Bordeaux Index, Liberty Wines, 12% abv (page 28)

- 2011 Soave, Vignale, Veneto, Italy, £4.99, Waitrose, 12%
- 2010 Txomín Etxaníz Getaria (Txakolí), Getariako Txakolina, País Vasco, Spain, £19.99, The Oxford Wine Company, 11.5% abv (page 34)
- 2011 Viña Esmeralda, Torres, Cataluña, Spain, c.£8.15, Waitrose, 11.5%
- 2011 Viña Sol, Torres, Catalunya, Spain, £6.29, Asda, 11.5% abv (page 85)
- 2010 Vinho Verde Branco, Loureiro, Afros, Portugal, £12.49, Les Caves de Pyrène, 12%
- 2011 Vinho Verde, Quinta de Azevedo, Sogrape, Minho, Portugal, £7.25-£6.75, Majestic, Oddbins, Stevens Garnier, Waitrose, The Wine Society, 11% (page 68)

Rosé wine
- 2010 Cabernet Rosé, Nagyréde Estate, Mátra, Hungary, £5.79, Booths,12% (page 103)
- 2011 Cuvée Fleur, Vin de France, £4.69, Waitrose, 12%
- 2011 English Rosé (Chapel Down), £11.99, M&S, 11%
- 2009 Grenache Rosé, Plume, Domaine la Colombette, VdP des Coteaux du Libron, Languedoc-Roussillon, France, £6.29, Booths, 9%
- 2011 Pinot Rosé, VdP du Pays d'Oc, Domaine Begude, Languedoc, France, £8.99, Majestic, 11.5%
- 2011 Rosé d'Anjou, Champteloup, Loire Valley, France, £7.99, Waitrose, 11%
- 2010 Rosé, Toro Loco, Utiel-Requena, Valencia, Spain, £3.59, Aldi, 12% (page 103)
- 2010 Txakoli Rosado, Ameztoi, País Vasco, Spain, £12.99, Les Caves de Pyrène, 10.5%

Red wine
- 2010 Cheverny Rouge, Clos du Tue-Boeuf, Loire Valley, France, £13.49, Les Caves de Pyrène, 11.5%
- 2011 Côte Roannaise, Domaine Robert Sérol, Loire Valley, France, £10.55, Christopher Piper, 12%
- 2011 Cuvée Chasseur, Vin de France, Les Producteurs Réunis, £4.69, Waitrose, 12% (page 96)
- 2011 Cuvée de Richard, VdP du Pays d'Aude, Languedoc-Roussillon, France, £5.29, Majestic, 12%
- 2011 El Guia Tinto, Bodegas Borsao, Utiel-Requena, Spain, £3.99, Waitrose, 12% abv (page 96)
- 2010 Gamay, Mon Cher, Noëlla Morantin, Loire Valley, France, £16.99, Les Caves de Pyrène, 12%
- 2011 Gamay, VdP de l'Ardèche, Cave de St-Désirat, Rhône Valley, France, £4.99, M&S, 12% (page 95)
- 2011 Marzemino delle Venezie, Sainsbury's Taste the Difference, Italy, £5.99, Sainsbury's, 12%
- 2009 Mauvais Temps, VdP de l'Aveyron, Domaine Nicolas Carmarens, Southwest France, £18.99, Caves de Pyrène, 11.5%
- 2010 Negroamaro del Salento, La Casada Caleo, Puglia, Italy, £8.49, Caves de Pyrène, 12%
- 2011 Reggiano Rosso, Emilia-Romagna, Italy, £5.99, M&S, 12%
- NV Sainsbury's House Beaujolais, France, £4.79, Sainsbury's, 12% abv (page 95)
- 2010 Syrah, VdP de l'Ardèche, Hervé Souhaut, Domaine Romaneaux-Destezet, France, £21.99, Les Caves de Pyrène, 11.5% abv (page 42)
- 2011 Trinacria Rosso, Sicily, Italy, £3.99, Waitrose, 12%
- NV Sainsbury's House Valpolicella, Veneto, Italy, £4.49, Sainsbury's, 12%
- 2011 Valpolicella, Vignale, Veneto, Italy, £5.49, Waitrose, 12%

fizz

If we couldn't all start drinking fizz in a year like 2012, there's no hope for us. The Queen's Diamond Jubilee, the Olympics... Chelsea winning the Champions League, come to that. Yet there was one more celebration that may have got swamped in the regal, Olympian rush, but one that was still of supreme importance. The year 2012 was the 350th anniversary of the invention of Champagne. Or perhaps I should rephrase that: the 350th anniversary of the invention of the 'Champagne method' of making wine sparkle by inducing a second fermentation in the bottle. And this wasn't achieved by a Frenchman; it was a 'hearts of oak' Englishman, Christopher Merret. So don't let the French tell you otherwise: the English invented Champagne, not the French. Luckily the quality of fizz has been well up this year. Champagne brands have made more effort and there are some very good big-name offerings in the ice buckets. At the budget bubbles level, there's lots of bright, breezy, happy-go-lucky Prosecco around. And as for England... as fate would have it, we're often drinking the results of the glorious 2009 vintage – remember that summer? English fizz has never been better, and God bless all of us.

• The wines are listed in descending price order.

2005 Champagne Le Mesnil, Blanc de Blancs, Grand Cru Brut, France, 12% abv

Waitrose, £32.99

The village of Le Mesnil grows what I think may be the greatest Chardonnay grapes in Champagne. And that is all that goes into this wine: Le Mesnil Chardonnay. Nothing else. Which explains why this gentle, foaming, creamy wine is always a genuine challenger in flavour to the glitzy, over-hyped *blanc de prestige cuvées*, and yet is only half the price. If you want to impress, don't throw your money at a pile of marketing blarney. Instead, tell the story of the chalk slopes of Le Mesnil, the perfect Chardonnay grapes and the tiny, tight-knit cooperative winery which, year by year, produces this soft, soothing marriage of fluffy apple flesh, dry, savoury toffee and farm-gate crème fraîche.

NV Champagne Herbert Beaufort, Bouzy Grand Cru Brut, France, 12% abv

M&S, £32

Powerhouse stuff. You don't go to the Pinot Noir village of Bouzy for delicacy and elegance. You go there for the biggest, burliest flavours in Champagne. This is uncompromising Champagne. The flavour is so intense you wonder if it's not quite dry. Don't worry; it's the sheer power of baked apples straight from the oven, apple pie with a scattering of raisins and dates, and chewy loft apples drowned in syrup. I know it sounds sweet; it isn't. And this applemania is tempered by toasted, salted hazelnuts, lemon-zest acidity and the savoury scent of leather. Oh, and if it grabs you, a kind of honeyed sweat. No? Well, you don't have to buy it.

2007 Gusbourne Blanc de Blancs, English Sparkling Wine, Gusbourne Estate, Kent, England, 12% abv
armit, £29.99

The label proclaims *méthode Anglaise* – as opposed to *méthode champenoise.* Well, that's OK. We'll need to be taking swipes at poor old Champagne for a few years yet as we struggle to assert our primacy in the sparkling-wine stakes – and we *did* invent the stuff. But just for now Gusbourne is attempting to claim the title of Kent's finest. I love it. We're developing regional differences: Kent is different from Sussex or Hampshire, and inside Kent (or Sussex, Hampshire, Dorset, wherever...), different estates are developing fantastically different styles to ones made a few miles down the road. I'm a Kent boy, I thought I knew the county, but I only discovered Gusborne a year ago. In 12 months' time I hope I'm saying the same thing about somewhere entirely different. Oh, the wine. It's excellent: it manages to be full and mellow, hazelnuts and apple pie slathered with crème fraîche, tempered by crisp, juicy acidity, and leaving a lingering yeasty, creamy aftertaste long after you've swallowed.

NV Champagne Henri Giraud, Esprit Brut, Henri Giraud, France, 12% abv
Selfridges, £29.99

Fascinating wine from the superstar village of Aÿ – that's where Bollinger is ensconced. Hardly anyone uses oak barrels nowadays in Champagne, but these guys use small barrels from the Argonne forest. It makes a difference. The wine has a mildly floral scent, and a certain spring-awakening, forest sappiness that is a delight. The squashy fresh fruit is more greengage plums and melon rather than the usual apples, and it's all wrapped round with savoury hazelnut and cream.

2007 Nyetimber Classic Cuvée Sparkling Wine, Nyetimber, West Sussex, England, 12% abv
Waitrose, £29.99

Nyetimber was founded by a couple of feisty Chicagoans, but it has evolved to become the proud standard-bearer for world-class English sparkling wine. It was excellent when the Americans made it, but the new generation of winemakers, allied to new vineyards in some of the most promising parts of southern England, has added a purity of flavour, an almost

fizz

- There's a tongue-tingling, mouth-watering purity about good English sparkling that often outclasses a similarly priced Champagne. In Jubilee/Olympics year 2012, we increasingly turned to home-grown fizz for celebration.
- Despite last summer, England is naturally suited to grow grapes for sparkling wine.
- Look for Balfour, Breaky Bottom, Camel Valley, Denbies, Gusbourne, Nyetimber and Ridgeview.

linear determination of character – necessary when you're trying to persuade the world your wine is better than Champagne – and a coating of gentleness as tasty as the best French crème fraîche. Well, that's something to keep the French happy, but the purity, the proudness of this wine is utterly English: ripe and crisp English apples, pure leafy acidity scented with lemon verbena, wrapped in hazelnut cream and apple-pie pastry. I tasted this again after some very good Champagnes, and it was just so pure, so focused, and so proud that it makes you proud to be a Brit.

NV The Society's Champagne, Private Cuvée, Brut, Alfred Gratien, France, 12.5% abv

The Wine Society, £27

Continuity. Consistency. Serenity. The Society's Champagne floats blithely along, always delivering its utterly reassuring, slightly old-fashioned style. I'm sure it was much the same at the Queen's Silver Jubilee, at her Coronation... at her birth, for all I know. Certainly, as long as I can remember, this wine has been a gentle, foaming mix of apples, nuts, cream and brioche crust, with perhaps a touch of tarte tatin richness that is a delight now but will happily – indeed, enthusiastically – age for another 10 years.

NV Champagne Alexandre Bonnet, Brut Rosé, France, 12% abv

Waitrose, £26.99

The ripest black Pinot Noir grapes in Champagne are grown in the far south of the region, and one tiny area in particular actually specializes in a dense, muscular, still, dry Pinot Noir rosé – Rosé de Riceys – no bubbles, but tons of flavour. With the grapes that don't go into that, M. Bonnet makes some of the fullest, roundest, but best-balanced fizzy rosés in Champagne. Some rosés can be very pale and lean – not this one. It has a slightly syrupy ripeness to it, lapping over a dishful of ripe strawberry and peach fruit, brioche bread crust and a creaminess indulgently balanced between crème brûlée and good old English custard (from the tin, of course).

NV Champagne Delamotte Brut, France, 12% abv

Corney & Barrow, £26.50
There was a time when I hung out with chefs – not a good idea, but you have to learn the hard way – and we drank Delamotte. Bottle after bottle after bottle. And the reason was it had such a pure taste. A lot of Champagne leaves you wondering when the hangover will start, but with Delamotte it often didn't. The grapes are from my favourite Champagne Chardonnay village, Le Mesnil-sur-Oger, where the ripe apple fruit sinks into a creaminess like rice pudding dashed with honey, and the fresh acidity says 'Drink me now, but if you can wait a few years, so can I.'

NV Champagne Jacquart Brut Mosaïque, France, 12.5% abv

Great Western Wine, £25
They call this Mosaïque because it's made up of different wines from a whole mosaic of vineyards in the two best Champagne zones – the Montagne de Reims and the Côtes des Blancs – and most of them are *grand cru* or *premier cru*, the top sites. But that's not all. This is a non-vintage wine, and 20 per cent of the blend is of old reserve wines kept back to add richness. Add to that a period of three to four years when the wine lies on its yeast lees, soaking up the creamy softness they exude, and... Well, you'll be getting thirsty. But it really works. There are so many mellow flavours flickering in and out of the wine: white bread crust, or is it yeasty dough? Probably both. Baked cream, milk chocolate or crème fraîche? All three. Biscuits, fluffy apples, a friendly foaming cascade of bubbles... very good stuff.

fizz

2009 Blanc de Blancs Brut, Marksman, Ridgeview Wine Estate, West Sussex, England, 12.5% abv
M&S, £22

This delightful 100 per cent Chardonnay from the Sussex Downs shows the gorgeous quality of 2009. It's made by Ridgeview, and they've used just a tiny bit of French oak barrel-ageing to give the wine spice and a dash of vanilla cream. It works. This has a gurgling, foaming bubble, an underpinning of mouth-watering rather than raw acidity, which is the mark of good English fizz, and a mellow softness that veers between butter croissants, brioche and cream cake, but probably opts for the classic Champagne brioche as a semi-respectful touch of the forelock to the fizz-makers across the Channel.

NV Premier Cru Champagne Brut, Tesco Finest, Union Champagne, France, 12.5% abv
Tesco, £20.99

I have to take my hat off to Tesco for this. Year on year, it's a relentlessly consistent glass of Champagne that always reflects the high-quality, chalky slopes around Avize, one of the Côte de Blancs' best villages. It's direct, fresh, attractively creamy, with just a little nut syrup to balance the acidity and a rolling foaming cascade of soft bubbles.

• If you want a slightly more intense version from the same village, Haynes, Hanson & Clark will supply **Pierre Vaudon Brut** for £25.90.

NV Quartet Anderson Valley Brut, Roederer Estate, Anderson Valley, California, 12% abv
Oddbins, £20

Many people think that Roederer is the best of all the big Champagne producers in France, but the company has never been parochial and smug in its approach to fizz. Roederer pioneered sparkling production in Tasmania at what's now the excellent Jansz operation, and chose the windiest, foggiest, dampest part of California to make bubbles, because its winemakers said it reminded them so closely of the pretty ornery conditions they have to endure back home in France. They make a variety of superb California wines – mostly snapped up as soon as they leave the winery – but we Brits do get some Quartet. It's a joy: a foaming but well-behaved riot of brioche and Chelsea buns dusted with icing sugar, dashed with cream and cut with just enough acidity, like lemon juice in a fruit salad, and tinged by the soothing aroma of a cup of Horlicks cooling in the next room.

NV Pelorus Brut, Cloudy Bay, Marlborough, New Zealand, 12.5% abv

Waitrose £19.99

This is one of the stars of the Southern Hemisphere. It's the sparkling wine of the famous Cloudy Bay, but I prefer to call it Veuve Clicquot's Southern arm. Year by year it produces sophisticated, elegant, beautifully balanced sparklers. Year by year I fret about Veuve Clicquot's style and quality going up and down like a yo-yo. Why? Is there less sales and marketing pressure on Pelorus?

Is Veuve Clicquot heavily involved with brand image, while Pelorus just gets on with making smashing wine? Whatever the reason, Pelorus is fabulous, complex, fascinating fizz. It's full, dry; its bubbles foam rather than crackle and its fruit is ripe apple streaked with lemon zest and green apple peel. But it's the creamy, nutty flavours that make exciting Champagne, and they're on parade in this sparkling wine: cashews and hazelnuts, dry French *biscottes*, Puffed Wheat, Ovaltine and the tangy, meaty delight of Twiglets. Hmmm. Can you really make a wine taste like a breakfast cereal brand, a nightcap drink brand and everyone's favourite party nibble?

NV Valdobbiadene Prosecco Superiore, Sorelle Branca, Veneto, Italy, 11% abv

Harvey Nichols, £15

This is Prosecco wearing a diamond tiara and a string of pearls. Class isn't *de rigueur* with Prosecco, but here we get it anyway, right from the cool, black-and-silver label showing a night sky and a flock of birds lit up by the bright, full moon. There's just a bit more of everything here: more apple-blossom scent, more uplifting flavour of pear with just a hint of banana, and an acidity fresh yet soft like the rind of a parboiled lemon. How entirely correct that the ladies who congregate in the elegant Fifth Floor bar in the London store should have the best Prosecco with which to dally.

NV Sparkling Burgundy Blanc de Blancs, Crémant de Bourgogne, Cave de Lugny, Burgundy, France, 11.5% abv
Waitrose, £11.99
They say (well, I do, quite often) that sparkling Burgundy (Crémant de Bourgogne) is the closest the French get to Champagne but at half the price. That makes sense. Burgundy uses the same Chardonnay and Pinot Noir grapes, and uses the 'Champagne method' to make the wine. But this particular blend, for once, doesn't taste like Champagne at all. It's got a zingy, green-apple fruit and a snappy smell of blackcurrant leaves and coffee beans. The texture is a bit more Champagne-like – round and full and slightly creamy – but it's the attractive fresh, green, streaked fruit and perfume that will have me finishing one glass and enthusiastically reaching for another.

NV Crémant de Limoux Brut, Cuvée Royale, Limoux, France, 12% abv
Waitrose, £10.99
Modern Crémant de Limoux is very different from the Blanquette de Limoux which, for generations, was southern France's only decent fizz. Those Blanquettes were marked by powerful, green-apple flavours from the local Mauzac grape. But if there is any apple in modern *crémant* it's of a soft, ripe, fluffy-textured kind, not at all gum-challenging. The overriding feeling is of a mellow creaminess, a soft, foaming bubble, and even a hint of fruit syrup – that'd be apple.

NV Prosecco, Bisol, Veneto, Italy, 11.5% abv
Tesco, £9.99
This seems to be the target price for Prosecco this year. When you consider we'd not even heard of Prosecco a few short years ago and were all using Cava for our parties (at several pounds a bottle less), this almost a tenner a stuff

had better be good. Well, it is. The £9.99 Proseccos have a bit more freshness and fruit than last year, with pear and banana fruit pleasing your palate while the bubbles lift your spirits.

• **Il Papavero** (Laithwaite's, £9.99) and **San Leo** (Waitrose, £9.49) are also good.

NV Cava Brut, Metodo Tradicional, Penedès, Cataluña, Spain, 11.5% abv
Morrisons, £6.99

You can get cheaper Cava, but since you're supposed to be enjoying yourself (not clutching your gut), getting the cheapest available is sometimes a false economy. This is decent, traditional Cava, without any tarting up. It's mild – not a bad thing with cheap Cava – and has a reasonable creamy flavour made more savoury by something like sausage meat (that's a compliment; good Champagne and good white Burgundy can have a sense of sausage meat) and with just enough peppery bite to sharpen it up.

NV Cava Rosado, Metodo Tradicional, Penedès, Cataluña, Spain, 12% abv
Morrisons, £6.99

I could have lumped this pink Cava in with the Morrisons white version (above), but I wanted to make the point that pink Cava is usually better than the equivalent white version, and the same price. This is better than the white. It's quite mature, with a definite flavour of strawberries (always a good sign) in this case mixed in with some apple purée, a little chewy peach skin, and all this is kept sharp by the typical Cava streak of metal and apple peel.

• Asda's **Mas Miralda Cava Rosado** isn't bad at £4.49, and **Codorníu Rosado** (Tesco, £9.96) is quite classy.

NV Valdobbiadene Prosecco Superiore, Veneto, Italy, 11% abv
Aldi, £6.99

Prosecco is not really cheap party pop. Most of it is in the £9-£11 bracket, and we seem to be prepared to pay the extra because it's so good at getting the party spirit going. But you can still get pretty good Prosecco for less – and, as usual, the bargain-hunter's friend, Aldi, delivers the goods with this wine. This has a nice slightly floral smell and a good slightly sharp pear flavour. It'll do the trick.

• Aldi also does **Crémant de Jura** – another good, soft, less fruity sparkler for £6.99.

fortifieds

And there's me thinking that *Downton Abbey* would surely see a surge of interest in sophisticated drinks such as Sherry and Port. Indeed, I'd heard that the '*Downton* effect' was causing increased Sherry consumption across the land – it was at M&S – and I've enthusiastically patronized various of the Sherry-dominated Spanish bars that have started to pop out of the woodwork – and they seemed to be packed and lively when I was trying to get a drink at the bar. On a more rarefied note, the most exciting event I went to last year at the giant Vinexpo Wine Fair was a tasting of 'En Rama' (Limited Edition) sherries from González Byass: sherries drawn off the barrel, not stabilized or filtered, just dashed into a bottle and rushed to market – fabulous, fascinating flavours that sell out as soon as they hit our shelves (Lea & Sandeman is a good bet if you want to try them, but you'll have to hurry: once they arrive a couple of times each year, they're gone). But other supermarkets and merchants seem strangely uninterested in showing us their fortified-wine ranges in their tastings, as though they've resigned themselves to the fact that fewer and fewer (and older and older) people are buying these beauties. Funny; the people I saw mobbing the bar in the new Spanish places were almost all young. The people who collar me at tastings to talk about Port are almost all young. So, for the young – at heart, and on the birth certificate – here are some of the best.

• In this section you will find sherries first, then ports, followed by Madeira and Marsala, in descending order of price.

SHERRY

Delicado Fino Sherry, González Byass, Spain, 15.5% abv
Waitrose, £13.99/50cl
González Byass makes the excellent, world-famous Tio Pepe fino: pale, dry and refreshing. This is a wine of similar quality that has been aged for a couple of years longer in big barrels and so is a little darker in colour, a little fuller in flavour, and definitely more austere in style, despite its fullness. The scrubbed-clean but careworn smell of old banisters and creaky old stairways climbing to nowhere at the top of an empty house... that's the smell. If you know it, you won't forget it, and you can find it here.

Dry Oloroso Sherry, Solera Jerezana, Emilio Lustau, Spain, 20% abv,
Waitrose, £8.99
This is almost totally dry, but not quite, yet the final effect is impressive. It has that wonderful, rather dangerous smell that good Sherry gives off – as though someone had splashed a little balsamic vinegar in the barrel – and this gives notice that the wine is going to be just a bit wild and assertive.

Thank goodness. True oloroso Sherry which matures in barrel in contact with the air is not for faint hearts. That balsamic acid transforms on your palate into the acid of an old bottle of cider, which reacts brilliantly with the figs and dates and sultanas, the fruit cake and the crunchy hazelnuts and almonds that all crowd together in a chewy, rich, even syrupy melange that coats your mouth at the same time as challenging your palate.
• **Waitrose Dry Amontillado** (£8.99) is also very good.

Dry Old Palo Cortado, Emilio Lustau, Spain, 19% abv
M&S, £7.49/37.5cl
This is a wonderful, very rare style of Sherry that inhabits a chestnut-tinted no-man's land between fino and oloroso. The Lustau company laid down 35 barrels of this wine in the 1930s, and every year they draw a little off and replace it with young wine. So there's a bit – not much, but a bit – of wine from

the 1930s in this bottle. And it's a delight: full, dry, but with a rounded, slightly buttered Brazils, caramel-and-nut taste; the nuts are chewy, the caramel bone-dry, as dry as the raisins are, but not quite as dry as the gaunt old wood of the barrels from the 1930s.

• **Waitrose Palo Cortado** (£8.99) is also very good.

Manzanilla Sherry, Williams & Humbert, Spain, 15% abv
M&S, £6.99

The driest and leanest of the high-street manzanillas – but that's praise, not criticism, because the best manzanilla is light, almost water white, and ideally flecked by the salty sea breeze that whips in off the waves at Sanlúcar where the wine is made. This has the classic soft yet creamy flavour of bread dough full of yeast before it's put in the oven, but also something subtly different: the uncooked dough of scones. The fresh acidity is tantalizing, darting through

the wine, and if it has fruit, it's the chewy fruit of a green apple core.

Special Reserve Manzanilla, Tesco Finest, Bodegas Barbadillo, Spain, 15% abv
Tesco, £5.79/50cl

This is good, bone-dry Sherry, but it doesn't initially have that savoury, salty tang which is such a delight in manzanilla wine matured by the seaside in Sanlúcar. It seems a bit fuller and rounder than I'd expect – more like a fino from inland Jerez,

fortifieds

and I almost found the kind of Brazil nut softness I'd expect in a dry amontillado for a moment. But the manzanilla flavour does arrive if you hold the wine in your mouth for a bit. There's a splash of sour cream, some fresh-roasted almonds, the murmuring rasp of pebbles... and there it is: the savoury saltiness of seaside manzanilla. At last.

Special Reserve Oloroso, Tesco Finest, Bodegas Barbadillo, Spain, 19% abv
Tesco, £5.79/50cl

There was a time when you'd reckon Tesco would be the first to sweeten and soften up an oloroso to give it mass-market appeal. Well, clearly that view doesn't hold with the buyers in charge of the 'Finest' range because this is bone-dry, almost peppery, with an aggressive, black-chocolate bitterness that would go brilliantly with chorizo and Pata Negra ham. But there's much

more to the flavour than just austere aggression; there's a dense richness of Fowler's black treacle, raisins, prunes – black figs cut through with acidity, and only softened by an impressive kind of multigrain, dark-brown-bread maltiness mixed with baked toffee and nuts.

The Society's Fino, Sánchez Romate, Spain, 15% abv
The Wine Society, £5.75

The first thing I would say is that The Wine Society's fino is still one of the greatest bargains in the world of wine. The second thing I would say is that they seem to have softened it into a rather 'British cold-climate' style, as though the previously marvellously austere style was deemed a bit severe for us shivering Brits. Well, I suppose they know their members, but I would be surprised if they wanted their fino fatter and waxier. Don't get me wrong; this is still good fino, which is, in any case, a fuller style than manzanilla, and it does have good touches of uncooked pastry dough, Brazil and hazelnuts and a faint slightly sour acid nip. It is properly dry. And it is a great price. It's just that, well...

PORT

1999 Quinta dos Malvedos Vintage Port, W & J Graham, Portugal, 20% abv

Tanners Wine Merchants, The Wine Company, £32.99–£32.20

Although 1999 is not a famous vintage, the quality of the Malvedos vineyard is so high, and the care and commitment lavished on it by Graham is so considerable that I think I could say that this producer never makes a bad Malvedos. In the great vintages this forms the core of the Graham's vintage Port, but in lighter vintages, the vineyard's grapes are kept separate and bottled as a single-vineyard wine. So here you get the real quintessence of Malvedos: a dark, dense wine, powerful, spicy and serious. The fruit is rich blackberry, fattened with chocolate and given a good, bitter, licorice edge. The spices are those great co-conspirators, cinnamon, ginger and clove; only nutmeg is missing from the perfect Christmas punch recipe. Drink this instead – this Christmas or for at least another 10 Christmases to come.

2001 Taylor's Vargellas Vintage Port, Taylor, Fladgate & Yeatman, Portugal, 20.5% abv

Fortnum & Mason, Majestic, Selfridges, Tesco, Waitrose, £32.50–£26.99

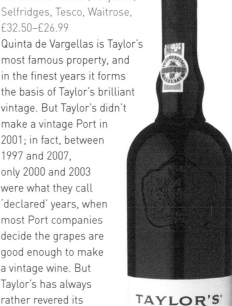

Quinta de Vargellas is Taylor's most famous property, and in the finest years it forms the basis of Taylor's brilliant vintage. But Taylor's didn't make a vintage Port in 2001; in fact, between 1997 and 2007, only 2000 and 2003 were what they call 'declared' years, when most Port companies decide the grapes are good enough to make a vintage wine. But Taylor's has always rather revered its Vargellas property, and since 1958 it has been released as a single-vineyard wine whenever it wasn't needed to provide pure class for the vintage wine. This isn't that deep in Port terms, but it's wonderfully scented and its texture is so mellow and smooth that it floats across your palate. There's a floral, almost violet scent which seamlessly joins the sweet blueberry and blackberry coulis fruit and the trails of herbs and spice that linger in the wine. It's lovely now, but this one will easily age 10 years.

1996 Vintage Port, Fonseca Guimaraens, Portugal, 20.5% abv
Selfridges, £32.99, Waitrose, 24.69

You wouldn't find Fonseca Port from a top vintage at this price, but when you see 'Fonseca Guimaraens' on the label of a vintage wine, it means it comes from a harvest of grapes that didn't quite make the highest grade. But the Fonseca style is still there, if in lighter

tones. Well, there's lighter and lighter. This is still as deep and dense as most people would want their port to be. It has luscious, pure, dark fruit whose flavour veers between blackberry and loganberry, and whose texture veers between an expertly reduced fruit sauce and homemade jam. There's some herb and pepper seasoning, too, and that's positively welcome in a lush, rich wine like this.

2003 Crusted Port, Graham's, Portugal, 20% abv
Sainsbury's, Tesco £18.99

Graham's is one of the top Port houses and by buying its crusted Port, you get a glimpse of its vintage Port, but at a fraction of the price. Graham's is famous for the sweet purity of its fruit and this one is beautifully mature, with lush blackberries and blackcurrants coursing joyously through the wine. There is a little tannic bitterness, but it is so smothered with dark fruit syrup.

NV Fonseca Terra Prima Reserve Port from Organically Grown Grapes, Fonseca Guimaraens, Portugal, 20% abv

Booths, £15.19, Vintage Roots, £16.50, Waitrose, £16.49

It's the perfume that makes this wine special, and if that's as a result of the organic farming of the grapes... I'm all for it. This really does have a heady scent, a dark-purple floral perfume and the sweet autumn scent of super-ripe damsons and blackberries being boiled up for jam in the kitchen. It's quite a tannic wine – it grips your tongue a bit – but the lush black plum and blackberry syrup laced with spice easily overcome any bitter streak. That said, you could age it for 10 years if you wanted to.

Port styles

- **Ruby** The youngest red Port with only 1–3 years' age.
- **Late Bottled Vintage (LBV)** Matured for 4–6 years in cask and vat, then usually filtered to avoid sediment forming. Unfiltered wines are labelled as such.
- **Tawny** Avoid cheap tawny. Aged tawny is matured in cask for 10–40 years before bottling, and older tawnies have delicious nut and fig flavours.
- **Vintage** The finest Port, matured in bottle, made from grapes from the best vineyards. Vintage Port is not 'declared' each year (usually 3–4 times per decade), and only during the second calendar year in cask if the shipper thinks standards are high enough.
- **White Port** Only the best taste dry and nutty from wood-ageing; most white ports are best served with tonic water and a slice of lemon.

Madeira

- This fortified wine is classified according to levels of sweetness. **Sercial** is the lightest and driest; **Verdelho** is slightly weightier and off-dry. **Bual** is fairly sweet and rich. **Malmsey** is very sweet.

- All madeiras get their pungent, smoky tang from they way they are aged, sometimes being artificially heated, sometimes just stored very warm, so that the wine gently oxidizes. It's not a flavour you'd welcome in other wines, but in Madeira it's essential.

2007 Late Bottled Vintage Unfiltered, Fonseca Guimaraens, Portugal, 20% abv

Cambridge Wine Merchants, £15.99, Selfridges, £17.99

That word 'unfiltered' is enormously important when it comes to LBV ports. 'LBV' means 'Late Bottled Vintage' – implying you're getting at least a version of the classy vintage style. But a lot of widely available and relentlessly advertised brands as well as the cheap own-labels are merely decent ruby ports aged for longer than usual and then tightly filtered to make them totally stable from Bedford to Brisbane. Character, they don't have. But this one, from the top-notch Fonseca operation, is based on high-quality grapes from a single harvest, aged in cask, and not filtered. The result is a wine full of lush texture and unctuous flavours that would have been left on the filter pad. There's more tannin and peppery spirit attack, too, but the wine can cope; that lush blackberry and blueberry richness, streaked through with fresh acid, takes any rough edges in its stride. And in any case, you could age this for five to 10 years, after which it really would be smooth.

MADEIRA

NV Madeira Bual 15-year-old, Henriques & Henriques, Portugal, 20% abv

Waitrose, £19.99/50cl

It would almost be easier simply to leave Madeira out of this guide; it's very difficult to find more than a token example, or none at all – on most wine merchants' lists, and it hardly ever features at tastings. Yet it is a special drink – a rare drink – I suppose you could call it a classic drink, since they've been making it for centuries and no one else has successfully copied it. Bual is a grape variety, and this wine is pretty sweet, but with good Madeira, sweet is a relative term, since acidity always plays a role. Here, the acidity is clear, slightly sour and chewy – like tamarind skin. Smokiness also plays its part, but not like a coal fire that won't draw properly; it's more like the fumes that hang around an old winery, and here they trail through a pageant of rich, brown flavours: dates, raisins, old brown wood and leather, homemade jam tarts burned in the oven and a rich glycerine syrup of all the fruits that ever began to lose their bloom and turn brown in the pantry of an Edwardian stately home.

MARSALA

NV Marsala Riserva Dolce 5-year-old, Martinez, Sicily, Italy, 18% abv

M&S, £6.49/37.5cl

Marsala is a Sicilian fortified wine that was famous for all the right reasons in the eighteenth and nineteenth centuries – i.e. it tasted good and lasted well on board Nelson's ships, but was famous for all the wrong reasons in the twentieth century – i.e. it made a mean zabaglione. By the twenty-first century it was all but forgotten. So I was amazed to find this tasty, worth-the-money example available in decent-sized M&S stores. It's chestnut-brown, not all that aromatic, but with a full, fat, rich grapiness that drifts into sultanas and dates and a brown, syrupy texture just lightly dabbed behind the ears with petrol.

fortified

sweeties

Sweet wine is not easy to make. In fact, good sweet wine probably takes more commitment, investment and luck than any other wine. The sweetness in the wine usually depends on an unlikely autumn combination of morning mist and lunchtime sunshine, which creates, against all the odds, a sublimely sweet kind of rot in the grapes – as opposed to 99 per cent of the other types of rot which simply turn the grape juice into vinegar. But this nectar-like juice will be in short supply; you'll have probably lost three-quarters of your crop searching for this 'noble rot'. Fermenting it, ageing it, stabilizing it so that it doesn't turn into a sweet-sour goo, and then trying to sell it... none of this is easy. And after all that, hardly anyone appreciates your final result. No wonder so many winemakers seem to keep back so much of their sweet wine for themselves. But making this beautiful, scented syrup obsesses winemakers. So, despite the fact that few merchants take sweet wine seriously, and also that few of us are eager to part with hard-won cash in tough times for the privilege of drinking it, here's a selection of the best, in the hope that a few of you will not be able to resist the lure of gold.

- The wines are listed in descending price order.
- Many sweet wines are sold in half-bottles (37.5cl) or 50cl bottles.

2008 Icewine, Gold Oak Aged Vidal, Inniskillin, Niagara Peninsula VQA, Ontario, Canada, 10% abv

Liberty Wines, £51.99/37.5cl
This is mad stuff. Thrilling, sensuous, delicious, but mad. Mad in price, mad in style. But if you live on the edge, and are in the mood for the wicked and the wild, well... here goes. This is the great Canadian speciality icewine – made from frozen grapes, picked in the drab dead of winter on the Niagara Peninsula. I've been there in December, and even wrapped up and centrally heated it's heavy on the soul. Out in the vines, bare-fingered and shivering to the core, you might question the human condition. And yet those tiny bullets of frozen Vidal grapes could just make it worthwhile because they transform into this: an orange-gold mayhem of strange, unexpected fruits led in the dance by quince and medlar, weaving in and out of the syrup of pineapple, strawberry and cling peaches (tinned), slapped with a leather flail, and all dripping with melted wax and honey. Wine's Pied Piper in ski pants and snowshoes. Go on, try it!

NV Muscat, All Saints Estate, Rutherglen, Victoria, Australia, 17% abv

Jascots (tel 020 8965 2000), £15.80/ 37.5cl
These deep, liqueur Muscats are some of the glories of Australia. They're not at all modern – when I first came across them you could virtually take a bucket to the winery and they'd fill it from the tap for a couple of quid. Now these wines are packaged in smart half-bottles and producers are charging a fair whack. And perhaps the wines are now a bit more sophisticated and elegant – but why would I want that? I want a faceful of hedonistic, of utterly irresistible Muscat grape heaven. Complexity of flavour, OK, but complicated, needing cogitation

and application of intellect? No. This one still has much of the old-time swagger about it, the rich, gooey sweetness of super-ripe Muscat grapes shrivelled on the vine. It has the suggestion of raisins and Christmas cake and dates, but it also has the scent of tea leaf and faded rose petals and cigars and a just-surviving freshness of orange peel.

- **Yalumba Museum Muscat** (Morrisons, £12.10/37.5 cl) and **Campbells Rutherglen Muscat** (Waitrose, £11.49/ 37.5 cl) are also good.

2009 Picolit, Colli Orientali del Friuli, Valbene, Paolo Valle & Alessandro Gallici, Friuli Venezia-Giulia, Italy, 13% abv
Laithwaite's, £14.99
Laithwaite's does pop up with some surprises when you're least expecting it. I'm not sure I've ever seen a Picolit wine available on the high street before – it's one of Italy's rarest sweet white wines, and it's historically very difficult to get the 'real thing', if you know what I mean. But here it is: a fascinating, orange-gold wine, with the richness of spun sugar, the chewy sweet-sourness of peach skins and a nip of bitter tamarind paste, all on a soft bed of doughnut crust sprinkled with summer dust instead of candy.

2008 Noble Late Harvest, Sauvignon Blanc, Mulderbosch, Stellenbosch, South Africa, 13% abv
armit, £14.99
South Africa is increasingly making green, tangy, sharp-fruited, dry Sauvignons to match those of New Zealand. But sweet Sauvignon is altogether a rarer beast. Somehow Sauvignon has a knack of keeping its flavour whatever you do to it, and this is bursting with green peppers, gooseberry, snow peas, greengage and lime – yet it has an oatmeal creaminess and whiff of woodsmoke and is beautifully, lusciously, sweet, glycerine sweet, syrup sweet, shot through with the green, green tastes of spring.

sweeties

1985 Rivesaltes Ambré Hors d'Age, Arnaud de Villeneuve, Roussillon, France, 16% abv

Waitrose, £13.99/50 cl

These old, wood-aged sweet wines from down near the Pyrenees are one of France's best-kept wine secrets. This wine was aged in small barrels and large vats for 20 years and then in bottle until now – and it's still only £13.99. But that's nothing. There are wines available on our market from 1962, 1950, 1946 – you name it – and not expensive. (Farr Vintners has details.) But start with this one: a dark, russet-tawny colour, a sweetness of shrivelled cherries, Victoria plums and goldengage plums beginning to change into raisins and dates but holding on to a youthful vigour – and after 20 years in a barrel – rather it than me – lush, deep, classy stuff.

2009 Sauternes, Tesco Finest, Yvon Mau, Sauternes, Bordeaux, France, 13.5% abv

Tesco, £12.99/37.5 cl

Since fine Sauternes is difficult and expensive to make, you don't expect to find top examples under a supermarket own-label. But sometimes a top property simply has a bit more wine in the cellar than it can sell, so well done, Tesco, for sniffing this one out. It comes from the well-respected Château Lamothe (the world-class Château Suduiraut lies in the same village) and this is spot-on Sauternes – the classic flavours of pineapple chunks soaked in syrup and butterscotch, promising to deepen to barley sugar with age, the texture of lanolin twined with glycerine, and the extra indulgence of a smear of crème fraîche straight from the local farm.

2011 Late Harvest Riesling, Waipara West, Waipara, New Zealand, 11% abv

Waterloo Wine Company, £12.50

Waipara West is one of New Zealand's most original wineries, perched along the banks of a raw, fast-flowing river miles from anywhere on the South Island. They've always made wine according to what they liked rather than what the marketeers said was needed, but who would heed a marketeer when you have the opportunity to make one of New Zealand's best sweet Rieslings? Riesling has a heavenly ability to encapsulate the fresh optimism of spring, the indulgent excess of a golden summer and the semi-fatigued, wistful end-game of autumn all in one sweet wine. This wine has a freshness of lemon blossom and an acidity as sharp as lime zest, at its heart is a mineral aspect as pure and glinting as warm riverbed stones in dry, high summer, and its fruit runs from spring to harvest: apple flesh turning from white to pink, honey as fresh as acacia and heather, a rich texture, and an autumnal syrup as warm as the dying sun.

• **Framingham** makes a richer, but equally beautiful **2011 Noble Riesling**, (Les Caves de Pyrène, £14.99/37.5 cl).

Enjoying sweeties

• Good sweet wines are difficult to make and not always easy to find, but please do try them as without lots of us buying them these delicious wines will no longer be made.

• Sweet wines can be enjoyed on their own. Savour their lusciousness. They also partner most puddings, especially fruit-based ones.

• Sauternes with Roquefort and other blue cheeses is a classic combination.

2009 Botrytis Semillon, Peter Lehmann, Barossa Valley, South Australia, 11.5% abv

Vin du Van, £10.75 (37.5 cl)
The Sémillon grape is at the heart of Sauternes, the sweet white wine from Bordeaux in France that many think of as the greatest dessert wine in the world. It isn't the sweetest – that's not the point; it's the lush, waxy texture that is so enthralling. And it's the Sémillon grape that imparts this treasure. Sémillon grows in numerous parts of the world, but almost always

sweeties

133

makes dry white wine – often waxy, but dry. Australia's Barossa Valley just occasionally manages to make it sweet, and it's a triumph: candle wax, beeswax, lanolin... how much more waxy texture could you want? This is swirled about with pineapple chunks and peaches steeped in honey while the whole mouthful is kept remarkably fresh with the sharp bite of lime zest and the leafy smell of rock dust in summer.

2010 Passito di Pantelleria Liquoroso, Pellegrino, Sicily, Italy, 15% abv
Oddbins, £10/37.5cl
I don't think anyone in Europe makes sweet Muscat much better than this. It comes from the island of Pantelleria, south of Sicily, which is actually closer to Africa than it is to Europe. This is a windswept, sun-soaked place, and the vines need to be buried in little craters to protect them from the gales. But the result is intensely sweet Muscat grapes, which are then left to dry and turn to raisins in the sun – and get even richer. This dessert wine triumphantly conserves the lush, scented essence of its Muscat grapes: baklava honey and grapes, nuts draped in syrup with a streak of lime for acidity and the satisfying sweet chewiness of orange rind in a top Dundee orange marmalade.

NV Floralis Moscatel Oro, Torres, Penedès, Cataluña, Spain, 15% abv
Majestic, £9.99, Morrisons, £8.13/50cl
This sweet wine was a new departure for the famous family firm of Torres not long ago. When first released it was very fresh, bright and floral. Now it seems to have entered a more solemn maturity –

perhaps sales were a little slow and stocks built up? – but it's just as good, more orange-gold in colour, with a rich, sultry texture and grapey sweetness dripping with syrup and beeswax to match the perfume of orange blossom and the blowsy scent of drooping hothouse blooms.

2005 Samos Anthemis, Vin de Liqueur, Samos, Greece, 15% abv

The Wine Society, £6.95/37.5 cl

I note this is a 2005 wine. It's always lovely to find a seven-year-old wine available for only £6.95, but maybe this is partly because no one can make head or tail of its labels. The front label is entirely in Greek or French, as is most of the back label, too, so if you don't know a) what Samos looks like spelled in Greek letters, or b) what Samos is in any case,

you're not going to be buying it. I don't know whether the rest of Greek exports suffer from this but, really, the Greeks could help themselves by making it simpler for us to buy their stuff. Well. Samos is one of Europe's most famous – yet understandably neglected – sweet Muscat wines. This isn't the greatest example I've enjoyed, but it's good: rich, and beginning to brown, with a round, waxy glycerine texture enveloping a sweetness that is moving away from grape and peach towards the darker world of stewed apricot, raisin and date.

NV Moscatel de Valencia, Cheste Agraria, Valencia, Spain, 15% abv

Asda, £4.13 /75 cl

Moscatel de Valencia has been the mainstay for a solid mouthful of grapey sweetness for so long that I registered a frisson of shock this year. It has changed. It has got better. It's not so thick and squodgy as it used to be. The grape juice and syrupy sweetness is still there: it's still fat and waxy, but it's actually starting to show a nip of acidity and a snappy suggestion of sharp grapefruit zest. Well, I never.

sweeties

STORING, SERVING AND TASTING

Wine is all about enjoyment, so don't let anyone make you anxious about opening, serving, tasting and storing it. Here are some tips to help you enjoy your wine all the more.

The corkscrew

The first step in tasting any wine is to extract the cork. Look for a corkscrew with an open spiral and a comfortable handle. The Screwpull brand is far and away the best, with a high-quality open spiral. 'Waiter's friend' corkscrews – the type you see used in restaurants – are good, too, once you get the knack. Corkscrews with a solid core that looks like a giant woodscrew tend to mash up delicate corks or get stuck in tough ones. And try to avoid those 'butterfly' corkscrews with the twin lever arms and a bottle opener on the end; they tend to leave cork crumbs floating in the wine.

Corks

Don't be a cork snob. The only requirements for the seal on a bottle of wine are that it should be hygienic, airtight, long-lasting and removable. Real cork is environmentally friendly, but is prone to shrinkage and infection, which can taint the wine. Synthetic closures modelled on the traditional cork are common in budget wines, but the largest increase has been in the use of screwcaps, or Stelvin closures, which are now appearing on some very classy wines, especially in Australia and New Zealand, South Africa and South America.

Laying down wine

The longer you intend to keep wine before you drink it, the more important it is to store it with care. If you haven't got a cellar, find a nook – under the stairs, a built-in cupboard or a disused fireplace – that is cool, relatively dark and vibration-free, in which you can store the bottles on their sides to keep the corks moist (if a cork dries out it will let air in and spoil the wine).

Wine should be kept cool – around 10–15°C/50–59°F. It is also important to avoid sudden temperature changes or extremes: a windowless garage or outhouse may be cool in summer but may freeze in winter. Exposure to light can ruin wine, but dark bottles go some way to protecting it from light.

Decanting

Transferring wine to a decanter brings it into contact with oxygen, which can open up the flavours. You don't need to do this ages before serving and you don't need a special decanter: a glass jug is just as good. And there's no reason why you shouldn't decant the wine to aerate it, then pour it back into its bottle to serve it. Some tough young wines can be transformed by this treatment, and red wines under screwcap also benefit from this.

Mature red wine is likely to contain sediment and needs careful handling. Stand the bottle upright for a day or two to let the sediment fall to the bottom. Open the wine carefully, and place a torch or candle beside the decanter. As you pour, stand so that

you can see the light shining through the neck of the bottle. Pour the wine into the decanter in one steady motion and stop when you see the sediment reaching the neck of the bottle.

Temperature

The temperature of wine has a bearing on its flavour. Heavy reds are happy at room temperature, but that phrase 'room temperature' was coined before central heating: 17–19°C/63–66°F is probably the max. The lighter the wine, the cooler it should be. I'd serve Burgundy and other Pinot Noir reds at cool larder temperature. Juicy, fruity young reds, such as wines from the Loire Valley, are refreshing served lightly chilled.

Chilling white wines makes them taste fresher, but also subdues flavours, so bear this in mind if you're splashing out on a top-quality white – don't keep it in the fridge too long. Sparkling wines, however, should be well chilled to avoid exploding corks and fountains of foam.

storing, serving & tasting

For quick chilling, fill a bucket with ice and cold water, plus a few spoonfuls of salt if you're in a real hurry. This is much more effective than ice on its own. If the wine is already cool, a vacuum-walled cooler will maintain the temperature.

The wine glass

The ideal wine glass is a fairly large tulip shape, made of fine, clear glass, with a slender stem. This shape helps to concentrate the aromas of the wine and to show off its colours and texture. For sparkling wine choose a tall, slender glass, as it helps the bubbles to last longer.

Look after your glasses carefully. Detergent residues or grease can affect the flavour of any wine and reduce the bubbliness of sparkling wine. Ideally, wash glasses in very hot water and don't use detergent at all. Rinse glasses thoroughly and allow them to air-dry. Store wine glasses upright to avoid trapping stale odours.

Keeping opened bottles

Exposure to oxygen causes wine to deteriorate, but most modern wines may actually improve after being open for a day. If you keep the opened bottle in the fridge, many wines can be delicious after one to two weeks. Recorking – or rescrewing the screwcap – is usually enough protection, but you can also buy perfectly effective devices to keep oxygen at bay if you want.

HOW TO TASTE WINE

If you just knock your wine back like a cold beer, you'll be missing most of whatever flavour it has to offer. Take a bit of time to pay attention to what you're tasting and I guarantee you'll enjoy the wine more.

Read the label

There's no law that says you have to make life hard for yourself when tasting wine. So have a look at what you're drinking and read the notes on the back label if there is one. The label will tell you the vintage, the region and/or the grape variety, the producer and the alcohol level.

Look at the wine

Pour the wine into a glass so it is a third full and tilt it against a white background so you can enjoy the range of colours in the wine. Is it dark or light? Is it viscous or watery? As you gain experience, the look of the wine will tell you one or two things about the age and the likely flavour and weight of the wine. As wine ages, whites lose their springtime greenness and gather deeper, golden hues, whereas red wines trade the purple of youth for a paler brick-red.

storing, serving & tasting

Swirl and sniff

Give the glass a vigorous swirl to wake up the aromas in the wine, stick your nose in and inhale gently. This is where you'll be hit by the amazing range of smells a wine can produce. Interpret them in any way that means something to you personally: it's only by reacting honestly to the taste and smell of a wine that you can build up a memory bank of flavours against which to judge future wines.

Take a sip

At last! It's time to drink the wine. So take a decent-sized slurp – enough to fill your mouth about a third full. The tongue can detect only very basic flavour elements: sweetness at the tip, acidity at the sides and bitterness at the back. The real business of tasting goes on in a cavity at the back of the mouth that is really part of the nose. The idea is to get the fumes from the wine to rise up into this nasal cavity. Note the toughness, acidity and sweetness of the wine, then suck some air through the wine to help the flavours on their way. Gently 'chew' the wine and let it coat your tongue, teeth, cheeks and gums. Jot down a few notes as you form your opinion and then make the final decision. Do you like it or don't you?

Swallow or spit it out

If you are tasting a lot of wines, you will have to spit as you go if you want to remain upright and retain your judgement. Otherwise, go ahead and swallow and enjoy the lovely aftertaste of the wine.

Wine faults

If you order wine in a restaurant and you find one of these faults, you are entitled to a replacement. Many retailers will also replace a faulty bottle if you return it the day after you open it, with your receipt. Some faults affect random bottles; others may ruin a whole case of wine.

- Cork taint – a horrible musty, mouldy smell indicates 'corked' wine, caused by a contaminated cork.
- Volatile acidity – pronounced vinegary or acetone smells.
- Oxidation – Sherry-like smells are not appropriate in red and white wines.
- Hydrogen sulphide – classic 'rotten eggs' smell.

Watch points

- Sediment in red wines makes for a gritty, woody mouthful. To avoid this, either decant the wine or simply pour it gently, leaving the last few centilitres of wine in the bottle.
- White crystals, or tartrates, on the cork or at the bottom of bottles of white wine are both harmless and flavourless.
- Sticky bottle neck – if wine has seeped past the cork it probably hasn't been very well kept and air might have got in. This may mean oxidized wine.
- Excess sulphur dioxide is sometimes noticeable as a smell of a recently struck match; it should dissipate after a few minutes.

storing, serving & tasting

141

wine style guide

When faced with a shelf – or a screen – packed with wines from around the world, where do you start? Well, if you're after a particular flavour, my guide to wine styles will point you in the right direction.

WHITE WINES

Bone-dry, neutral whites

Neutral wines nowadays aren't so neutral anymore. Good *sur lie* and especially good Chablis will have lemon, creamy yeast, and in Chablis' case, a lick of honey and real mineral bite. If you want really neutral wine Italian Pinot Grigio or cheap South African Chenin might be the best bets. But dry Italian whites have rocketed in quality recently and many have added scent and mineral flavours that didn't exist before. Better vineyard practices and better winemaking concentrate in putting more flavour in, not taking it out. The days when neutral whites existed as a mouthwash for the seafood or to avoid distracting you while you're eating are fading fast. Still, here are your best bets.

- Muscadet
- Chenin Blanc and Colombard – from the Loire Valley, Southwest France, Australia, California or South Africa
- Basic white Bordeaux and Entre-Deux-Mers
- Chablis
- Cheap southern French whites
- Pinot Grigio

Green, tangy whites

For nerve-tingling refreshment, Sauvignon Blanc is the classic grape, full of fresh green leaf, gooseberry and nettle flavours. I always used to go for New Zealand versions, but I'm now equally inclined to reach for a bottle from new-wave producers in Chile, South Africa or Hungary. Or even a simple white Bordeaux – Bordeaux Sauvignon is buzzing with life. Loire Valley Sauvignons can be overrated, but Touraine is often excellent. Austria's Grüner Veltliner has a peppery freshness. From northwest Spain, Galicia's Albariño grape has a stony, mineral lemon zest sharpness; the same grape is used in Portugal, for Vinho Verde. Alternatively, look at Riesling: Australia serves it up with aggressive lime and mineral flavours; New Zealand and Chile give milder versions of the same style. Alsace Riesling is lemony and dry, while German Rieslings go from bone-dry to intensely sweet, with the tangiest and zestiest coming from the Mosel Valley.

• Sauvignon Blanc – from New Zealand, Chile, Hungary, South Africa, or Bordeaux
• Loire Valley Sauvignons, especially Touraine, but also Sancerre and Pouilly-Fumé
• Riesling – from Australia, Austria, Chile, Germany, New Zealand, or Alsace in France
• Grüner Veltliner from Austria
• Vinho Verde from Portugal and Albariño from northwest Spain

Intense, nutty whites

The best white Burgundy from the Côte d'Or cannot be bettered for its combination of soft nut and oatmeal flavours, subtle, creamy oak and firm, dry structure. Prices are often hair-raising, but cheaper wines from single estates can offer a glimpse of real Burgundy style. For around £8–£10 your best bet is oaked Chardonnay from an innovative Spanish region such as Somontano, or around Limoux in Southwest France. You'll get a nutty, creamy taste and nectarine fruit with good oak-aged white Bordeaux or traditional white Rioja.

Top Chardonnays from New World countries – and Italy, for that matter – can emulate Burgundy, but we're looking at serious prices.

- White Burgundy – including Meursault, Pouilly-Fuissé, Chassagne-Montrachet, Puligny-Montrachet
- Oaked white Bordeaux – including Pessac-Léognan, Graves
- Oaked white Rioja
- Chardonnay from New Zealand and Oregon – and top examples from California and Australia (Western Australia and Victoria)

Ripe, toasty whites

Aussie Chardonnay conquered the world with its upfront flavours of peaches, apricots and melons, usually spiced up by the vanilla, toast and butterscotch richness of new oak. Good Aussie Chardonnays are now much more restrained, and this style has now become a standard-issue flavour produced by all sorts of countries, rarely to any great effect. You'll need to spend a bit more than a fiver nowadays if you want something to relish beyond the first glass. Oaked Australian Semillon can also give rich, ripe fruit flavours, as can oaked Chenin Blanc from South Africa. If you see the words 'unoaked' or 'cool-climate' on an Aussie bottle, expect an altogether leaner drink.

- Chardonnay: from Australia, Chile, California, South Africa, Spain
- Oak-aged Chenin Blanc from South Africa
- Australian Semillon

Aromatic whites

Alsace has always been a plentiful source of perfumed, dry or off-dry whites: Gewurztraminer with its rose and lychee scent or Muscat with its floral, hothouse grape perfume. A few producers in New Zealand, Australia, Chile and South Africa are having some success with these grapes. Floral, apricotty Viognier, traditionally the grape of Condrieu in the northern Rhône, now appears in *vin de pays* or IGP wines from all over southern France and also from California, Virginia and Australia. Condrieu is expensive (£20 will get you entry-level stuff and no guarantee that it will be fragrant); *vin de pays*/IGP wines start at around £5 and can be good. For aroma on a budget, grab some Hungarian Irsai Olivér or Argentinian Torrontés. English white wines often have a fresh, floral hedgerow scent – the Bacchus grape is one of the leaders of this style.

• Alsace whites, especially Gewurztraminer and Muscat
• Gewürztraminer from Austria, Chile, Germany, New Zealand and cooler regions of Australia
• Condrieu, from the Rhône Valley in France
• Viognier from southern France, Argentina, Australia, California, Chile, Virginia
• English white wines, especially Bacchus
• Irsai Olivér and Cserszegi Fűszeres from Hungary
• Torrontés from Argentina

Golden, sweet whites

Good sweet wines are difficult to make and therefore expensive: prices for Sauternes and Barsac (from Bordeaux) can go through the roof, but near-neighbours Monbazillac, Loupiac, Saussignac and Ste-Croix-du-Mont are more affordable. Sweet Loire wines such as Quarts de Chaume, Bonnezeaux and some Vouvrays have a quince aroma and a fresh acidity that can keep them lively for decades, as do sweet Rieslings such as Alsace Vendange Tardive, German and Austrian Beerenauslese (BA), Trockenbeerenauslese (TBA) and Eiswein. Canadian icewine is quite rare over here, but we're seeing more of Hungary's Tokaji, with its sweet-sour, marmalade flavours.

• Sauternes, Barsac, Loupiac, Ste-Croix-du-Mont
• Monbazillac, Saussignac, Jurançon and Pacherenc du Vic-Bilh from Southwest France
• Loire sweet whites such as Bonnezeaux, Quarts de Chaume and Vouvray *moelleux*
• Auslese, Beerenauslese and Trockenbeerenauslese from Germany and Austria
• Eiswein from Germany, icewine from Canada
• Botrytis Semillon, Riesling or Gewürztraminer from Australia, New Zealand and South Africa

RED WINES

Juicy, fruity reds

The definitive modern style for easy-going reds. Tasty, refreshing and delicious with or without food, they pack in loads of crunchy fruit while minimizing the tough, gum-drying tannins that characterize most traditional red wine styles. Beaujolais (made from the Gamay grape) is the prototype – and if you're distinctly underwhelmed by the very mention of the word 'Beaujolais', remember that the delightfully named Fleurie, St-Amour and Chiroubles also come from the Beaujolais region. Loire reds such as Chinon and Saumur-Champigny (made from Cabernet Franc) pack in the fresh raspberries. Italy's Bardolino is light and refreshing, as is young Valpolicella. Nowadays, high-tech producers all over the world are working the magic with a whole host of grape varieties. Carmenère, Malbec and Merlot are always good bets, and Grenache/Garnacha and Tempranillo usually come up with the goods. Italian grapes like Bonarda, Barbera and Sangiovese seem to double in succulence under Argentina's blazing sun. And at around £6–£7 even Cabernet Sauvignon – if it's from somewhere warm like Australia, South America, South Africa or Spain – or a *vin de pays* Syrah from southern France will emphasize the fruit and hold back on the tannin.

- Beaujolais – including Brouilly, Chiroubles, Fleurie, Juliénas, St-Amour. Also wines made from the Gamay grape in other parts of France
- Loire reds: Chinon, Saumur, Saumur-Champigny – and, if you're lucky, Bourgueil, Cheverny and St-Nicolas-de-Bourgueil
- Grenache (from France and Australia) and Garnacha (from Spain)
- Carmenère and Merlot from Chile
- Basic Merlot from just about anywhere
- Inexpensive Argentinian reds, especially Bonarda, but also Malbec, Sangiovese and Tempranillo

Silky, strawberryish reds

Here we're looking for some special qualities, specifically a gorgeously smooth texture and a heavenly fragrance of strawberries, raspberries or cherries. We're looking for soft, decadent, seductive wines. One grape – Pinot Noir – and one region – Burgundy – stand out, but prices are high to astronomical. Good red Burgundy is addictively hedonistic and all sorts of strange decaying aromas start to hover around the strawberries as the wine ages. Pinot Noirs from New Zealand, California, Oregon and cool parts of Australia such as Mornington Peninsula, Tasmania and Yarra Valley come close, but they're expensive, too; Chilean Pinots are far more affordable. You can get that strawberry perfume (though not the silky texture) from other grapes in Spain's Navarra, Rioja and up-coming regions like La Mancha and Aragón. Southern Rhône blends can deliver if you look for fairly light examples of Côtes du Rhône-Villages or Costières de Nîmes.

- Red Burgundy – including Volnay, Beaune, Nuits-St-Georges, Chambolle-Musigny, Givry
- Pinot Noir from Australia, California, Chile, New Zealand, Oregon
- Lightly oaked Spanish reds from Rioja, Navarra, La Mancha and Valdepeñas, especially with Tempranillo as the main grape
- Red blends from the southern Rhône Valley, such as Costières de Nîmes, Côtes du Rhône-Villages
- Australian Grenache from Barossa Valley and McLaren Vale
- Old-vine Cinsault

Intense, blackcurrant reds

Firm, intense wines that often only reveal their softer side with a bit of age; Cabernet Sauvignon is *the* grape, on its own or blended with Merlot or other varieties. Bordeaux is the classic region, and with global warming more and more producers can achieve this style, but some wines, especially from villages in the Haut-Médoc, need a few years to develop to a heavenly cassis and cedar maturity. Areas like St-Émilion and Pomerol will achieve this flavour more

Finding vegetarian and vegan wine

Virtually all wine is clarified with 'fining' agents, many of which are animal by-products. Although they are not present in the finished wine, they are clearly not acceptable for strict vegetarians and vegans. Alternatives such as bentonite clay are widely used and vegan wines rely solely on these; vegetarian wines can use egg whites or milk proteins.

- **Specialist merchants** Organic specialists such as Vintage Roots assess every wine on their lists for its vegetarian or vegan status.
- **Supermarkets** Most supermarkets stock some vegetarian and vegan wines and identify own-label ones with a symbol or 'V' logo.
- **Check the labels** Some producers, such as Chapoutier, use a 'V' symbol to indicate vegetarian wines. For others you may have to read the back label.

quickly. The rest of the world has moved to a riper, fruitier style. Chile does the fruity style par excellence. New Zealand can deliver Bordeaux-like flavours, but in a faster-maturing wine. Australia sometimes adds a medicinal eucalyptus twist, but can overripen the fruit to something approaching jam. Argentina and South Africa are making their mark, too. In Spain, Ribera del Duero can also come up with blackcurrant flavours, if the wines are not too ripe.

- Bordeaux reds such as Côtes de Castillon, St-Émilion, Pomerol, Moulis, Margaux, Pauillac and St-Julien
- Cabernet Sauvignon from just about anywhere
- Cabernet Sauvignon/Merlot blends

Spicy, warm-hearted reds

Australian Shiraz is the epitome of this rumbustious, riproaring style: dense, rich, chocolaty, sometimes with a twist of pepper, a whiff of smoke, or a slap of leather. But it's not alone. There are southern Italy's Primitivo and Nero d'Avola, California's Zinfandel and Petite Sirah, Mexico's Petite Sirah, Argentina's Malbec, South Africa's Pinotage, Toro from Spain and some magnificent Greek, Lebanese and Turkish reds. In southern France the wines of the Languedoc often show this kind of warmth, roughed up with hillside herbs. And if you want your spice more serious, more smoky and minerally, and sometimes with a floral scent, too, go for the classic wines of the northern Rhône Valley.

- Australian Shiraz, as well as blends of Shiraz with Grenache and Mourvèdre/ Mataro – and Durif
- Northern Rhône Syrah (Cornas, Côte-Rôtie, Hermitage, Crozes-Hermitage, St-Joseph) and southern Rhône blends such as Châteauneuf-du-Pape and Gigondas
- Southern French reds, such as Corbières, Fitou, Coteaux du Languedoc, Côtes du Roussillon, Faugères and Minervois
- Italian reds such as Primitivo, Aglianico, Negroamaro and Nero d'Avola
- Californian Zinfandel and Petite Sirah reds
- Argentinian Malbec
- South African Pinotage

Mouth-watering, sweet-sour reds

Sounds weird? This style is primarily the preserve of Italy, and it's all about food: the rasp of sourness cuts through rich, meaty food, with a lip-smacking tingle that works equally well with pizza or tomato-based pasta dishes. But there's fruit in there, too – cherries and plums – plus raisiny sweetness and a herby bite. The wines are now better made than ever, with more seductive fruit, but holding on to those fascinating flavours. All sorts of native Italian grape varieties deliver this delicious sour-cherries taste: Sangiovese (the classic red grape of Tuscany), Nebbiolo (from Piedmont), Barbera, Dolcetto, Teroldego, Sagrantino... You'll have to shell out at least a tenner for decent Chianti, more for Piedmont wines (especially Barolo and Barbaresco, so try Langhe instead). Valpolicella can be very good, especially Ripassos, but choose with care. Portugal reveals something of the same character in many of its reds.

- Chianti, plus other wines made from the Sangiovese grape, especially in Tuscany
- Barolo, Barbaresco and other wines made from the Nebbiolo grape
- Valpolicella Classico, Amarone della Valpolicella
- Southern Italian reds
- Dão, Alentejo, Tejo and other Portuguese reds

Delicate (and not-so-delicate) rosé

Dry rosé can be wonderful, with flavours of strawberries and maybe raspberries and rosehips, cherries, apples and herbs, too. Southern France and northern Italy are best for delicate pinks. Grapes like Cabernet, Syrah or Merlot give more flavour, or go for Grenache/Garnacha or Tempranillo from the Rhône Valley and Spain. South America is a good bet for flavoursome, fruit-forward pink wine. See pages 98–103 for my top pinks this year.

Why choose Fairtrade

By the time you've paid duty and VAT, and the retailer has taken their profit, there's often precious little left for the producer: if you buy a bottle of wine for £4.99, the producer gets, on average, under £1 – sometimes much less. The Fairtrade Labelling Initiative is a worldwide charitable organisation that works in partnership with producers in developing countries and guarantees a fair price for their products. Money is invested to help the growers and their communities to build a better future. You can be sure your money is doing good in the communities where the wine is produced. I've visited Fairtrade operations in South Africa, Argentina and Chile, and I always encourage them to keep quality up – as long as they do, we'll keep buying their wine.

- www.fairtrade.org.uk

SPARKLING WINES

Champagne can be the finest sparkling wine on the planet, but fizz made by the traditional Champagne method in Australia, New Zealand, England or California – usually using the same grape varieties – is often just as good and cheaper. It might be a little more fruity, where Champagne concentrates on bready, yeasty or nutty aromas, but a few are dead ringers for the classic style. Fizz is also made in other parts of France: Crémant de Bourgogne is one of the best. England is now beginning to rival Champagne in style. Italy's Prosecco is soft and delicately scented. Spain's Cava is available at bargain basement prices in all the big supermarkets, but pay a bit more and you'll get a much better wine.

• Champagne
• Traditional-method fizz made from Chardonnay, Pinot Noir and Pinot Meunier grapes grown in Australia, California, England, New Zealand, South Africa
• Crémant de Bourgogne, Crémant de Loire, Crémant de Jura, Crémant d'Alsace, Blanquette de Limoux
• Cava
• Prosecco
• Sekt is Germany's sparkling wine, and is occasionally 100 per cent Riesling
• Lambrusco from Italy is gently sparkling and usually red
• Sparkling Shiraz – an Aussie speciality – will make a splash at a wild party

FORTIFIED WINES

Tangy, appetizing fortified wines

To set your taste buds tingling, fino and manzanilla sherries are pale, perfumed, bone dry and bracingly tangy. True amontillado, dark and nutty, is also dry. Dry oloroso adds deep, raisiny flavours. Palo cortado falls between amontillado and oloroso; manzanilla pasada is an older, nuttier manzanilla. The driest style of Madeira, Sercial, is steely and smoky; Verdelho Madeira is a bit fuller and richer, but still tangy and dry.

- Manzanilla and fino Sherry
- Dry amontillado, palo cortado and dry oloroso Sherry
- Sercial and Verdelho Madeira

Rich, warming fortified wines

Raisins and brown sugar, dried figs and caramelized nuts – do you like the sound of that? Tawny ports and sweet Madeiras can offer you just that. Port is the classic dark, sweet wine, and it comes in several styles, from basic purple ruby, to tawny, matured in cask for 10 years or more, to rich, scented vintage, which matures to mellowness in the bottle. The Portuguese island of Madeira produces fortified wines with rich, brown, smoky flavours and a startling bite of acidity: the sweet styles to look for are Bual and Malmsey. Decent sweet sherries are rare; oloroso dulce is a style with stunningly concentrated flavours; PX is like treacle. In southern France, Banyuls, Rivesaltes and Maury are rich, deep, almost baked fortified wines. Marsala, from Sicily, has rich, brown sugar flavours with a refreshing sliver of acidity. The versatile Muscat grape makes luscious golden wines all around the Mediterranean, but also pops up in orange, black, and the gloriously rich, treacly brown versions that Australia does superbly.

- Port
- Bual and Malmsey Madeira
- Marsala
- Rich, sweet Sherry styles include Pedro Ximénez (PX), oloroso dulce

- *Vins doux naturels* from southern France: Banyuls, Maury, Rivesaltes
- Fortified (liqueur) Muscat 'stickies' from Australia. in particular from Rutherglen

Drink organic – or even biodynamic

- The widely discussed benefits of organic farming – respect for the environment, minimal chemical residues in our food and drink – apply to grapes as much as to any other produce. Full-blown organic viticulture forbids the use of synthetic fertilizers, herbicides or fungicides; instead, cover crops and companion planting encourage biodiversity and natural predators to keep the soil and vines healthy. Warm, dry climates like the South of France, Chile and South Africa have the advantage of rarely suffering from the damp that can cause rot, mildew and other problems – we should be seeing more organic wines from these regions. Organic wines from European countries are often labelled 'Biologique', or simply 'Bio'.
- Biodynamic viticulture takes working with nature one stage further: work in the vineyard is planned in accordance with the movements of the planets, moon, sun and cosmic forces to achieve health and balance in the soil and in the vine. Vines are treated with infusions of mineral, animal and plant materials, applied in homeopathic quantities, with some astonishing results.
- If you want to know more, the best companies to contact are Vinceremos and Vintage Roots (see pages 186–7).

wine style guide

buying wine for the long term

Most of this book is about wines to drink more or less immediately – that's how modern wines are made, and that's what you'll find in most high street and online retail outlets. If you're looking for a mature vintage of a great wine that's ready to drink – or are prepared to wait 10 years or more for a great vintage to reach its peak – specialist wine merchants will be able to help; the internet's another good place to look for mature wines. Here's my beginners' guide to buying wine for drinking over the longer term.

Auctions

A wine sale catalogue from one of the UK's auction houses will have wine enthusiasts drooling over names they certainly don't see every day. Better still, the lots are often of mature vintages that are ready to drink. Before you go, find out all you can about the producer and vintages described in the catalogue. My annually updated *Pocket Wine Book* is a good place to start, or *Michael Broadbent's Pocket Vintage Wine Companion* for old and rare wines; *Decanter*, the UK's leading consumer wine magazine, runs regular features on wine regions and their vintages. You can also learn a lot from tutored tastings – especially 'vertical' tastings, which compare different vintages. This is important, because some merchants take the opportunity to clear inferior vintages at auction.

The drawbacks? You have no guarantee that the wine has been well stored, and if it's faulty you have little chance of redress. As prices of the most sought-after wines have soared, so it has become profitable either to forge the bottles and their

GRAND VIN
DE
ATEAU LATOUR
REMIER GRAND CRU CLASSÉ
2000
PAUILLAC

contents or to try to pass off stock that is clearly out of condition. But for expensive and mature wines, I have to say that the top auction houses make a considerable effort to check the provenance and integrity of the wines. Don't forget that there will usually be a commission or buyers' premium to pay, so check out the small print in the sale catalogue. Online wine auctions have similar pros and cons.

If you've never bought wine at an auction before, a good place to start would be a local auctioneer such as Straker, Chadwick in Abergavenny (tel: 01873 852624, strakerchadwick.com) or Morphets in Harrogate (tel: 01423 530030, morphets.co.uk); they're less intimidating than the famous London houses of Christie's and Sotheby's and you may come away with some really exciting wine. Bonhams in London (bonhams.com) also has a thriving wine auction department.

Buying en primeur

En primeur is a French term for wine that is sold before it is bottled, sometimes referred to as a 'future'. In the spring after the vintage, the Bordeaux châteaux – and a few other wine-producing regions, particularly Burgundy and the top Rhône wines in good vintages – hold tastings of barrel samples for members of the international wine trade. The châteaux then offer a proportion of their production to the wine merchants (*négociants*) in Bordeaux, who in turn offer it to wine merchants around the world at an opening price.

The advantage to the châteaux is that their capital is not tied up in expensive stock for the next year

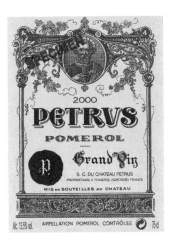

Wine for the future

There is a lot to be said for buying en primeur. For one thing, in a great vintage you may be able to find the finest and rarest wines far more cheaply than they will ever appear again. Every classic vintage in Bordeaux opens at a higher and higher price, but that price never permanently drops, and so the top wines increase in value, whatever price they start at. Equally, when a wine – even a relatively inexpensive one – is made in very limited quantities, buying en primeur may be practically your only chance of getting hold of it.

In the past, British wine merchants and their privileged customers were able to 'buy double what you want, sell half for double what you paid, and drink for free', but as the market has opened up to people more interested

or two, until the wines are bottled and ready to ship. Traditionally wine merchants would buy en primeur for stock to be sold later at a higher price, while offering their customers the chance to take advantage of the opening prices as well. The idea of private individuals investing in these wines rather than institutions took off with a series of good Bordeaux vintages in the 1980s; it's got ever more hectic since then and the stellar vintage of 2009 sent things ballistic as châteaux owners and investors tried to cash in on a wave of enthusiasm from China. Things have throttled back a bit since then.

in making a quick buck than drinking fine wine, the whole process has become more risky.

Another potential hazard is that a tasting assessment is difficult at an early date. There is a well-founded suspicion that many barrel samples are doctored (legally) to appeal to the most powerful consumer critics, in particular the American Robert Parker and the *Wine Spectator* magazine. The wine that is finally bottled may or may not bear a resemblance to what was tasted in the spring following the vintage. In any case, most serious red wines are in a difficult stage of their evolution in the spring, and with the best will in the world it is possible to get one's evaluation wrong. However, the aforementioned Americans, magazines like *Decanter*, the broadsheet newspapers and various blogs, will do their best to offer you accurate judgements on the newly offered wines, and most merchants who make a primeur offer also write a good assessment of the wines. You will find that many of them quote the Parker or *Wine Spectator* marks. Anything over 95 out of 100 risks being hyped and hiked in price. Many of the best bargains get marks between

85 and 89, since the 90+ marks are generally awarded for power rather than subtlety. Consideration can be given to the producer's reputation for consistency and to the general vintage assessment for the region.

Bordeaux swings and roundabouts

Prices can go down as well as up. They may not increase significantly for some years after the *en primeur* campaign. Some popular vintages are offered at ridiculously high prices, but it's only about twice a decade that the combination of high quality and fair prices offers the private buyer a chance of a guaranteed profit. Interestingly, if one highly touted vintage is followed by another, the prices for the second one often have to fall because the market simply will not accept two inflated price structures in a row. Recent Bordeaux examples of this are the excellent 2004 after the much-hyped 2003, and the fine 2001 after the understandably hyped 2000. Sadly this message doesn't always get through. Opening prices for 2005 were as much as 400% up on 2004 for the top wines. The less exciting 2006s dropped by a mere 15% from 2005's vastly inflated

level. The 2009 opened at historically high prices; the equally good 2010 opened even higher. No one was interested in 2011, even though some prices dropped by 30–50 per cent.

But the point to remember is that these crazy headline prices are for the top wines only. Modern Bordeaux makes more and more good red each year, and the prices rise modestly, if at all. So while top 2005s and 2009s might rise by £1000 a year per case, the vast majority, not overpraised by critics or craved by the affluent new Asian markets, have hardly moved, except for enforced changes due to currency changes such as a weak pound. Both 2009 and 2010 have been offered at record prices. But while for a top property that might mean savage increases, for lesser properties, the increase might only be a pound or two a bottle. In which case, do you really need to buy the current vintage *en primeur*? Not unless you are solely an investor. And even then you'd be better off buying top properties' wines from vintages like 2008 and 2006. These have been moving up in price appreciably, while 2009 and 2010 stagnate. If you want truly classic wine, buy 2005s. They seemed expensive when they were first offered; they now look positively cheap. Their prices will be on the move before long.

Secure cellarage
Another worry is that the merchant you buy the wine from may not still be around to deliver it to you two years later. Buy from a well-established

merchant you trust, with a solid trading base in other wines.

Once the wines are shipped you may want your merchant to store the wine for you; there is usually a charge of between £7 and £10 per case, per year, for this. If your merchant offers cellarage, you should insist that (1) you receive a stock certificate; (2) your wines are stored separately from the merchant's own stocks; and (3) your cases are identifiable as your property. All good merchants offer these safeguards as a minimum service.

Check the small print

Traditional wine merchants may quote prices exclusive of VAT and/or duty: wine may not be the bargain it first appears. A wine quoted *en primeur* is usually offered on an ex-cellars (EC) basis; the price excludes shipping, duties and taxes such as VAT. A price quoted in bond (IB) in the UK includes shipping, but excludes duties and taxes. Duty paid (DP) prices exclude VAT. You should check beforehand the exact terms of sale with your merchant, who will give you a projection of the final 'duty paid delivered' price.

retailers' directory

All these retailers have been chosen on the basis of the quality and interest of their lists. If you want to find a local retailer, turn to the Who's Where directory on page 192.
Case = 12 bottles

The following services are available where indicated:
C = cellarage   G = glass hire/loan   M = mail/online order   T = tastings and talks

A & B Vintners

Little Tawsden, Spout Lane, Brenchley, Kent TN12 7AS (01892) 724977 **fax** (01892) 722673 **email** info@abvintners.co.uk **website** www.abvintners.co.uk **hours** Mon–Fri 9–6 **cards** MasterCard, Visa; **delivery** 1–4 cases £12.50 + VAT within London; £16-19 M25 and Home Counties (postcode dependent); free for 5 cases or more within these areas; phone for information on other areas
minimum order 1 mixed case, **en primeur** Burgundy, Languedoc, Rhône. **C M T**
✪ *Specialists in Burgundy, the Rhône and southern France, with a string of top-quality domaines from all three regions.*

Adnams

head office & mail order Sole Bay Brewery, Southwold, Suffolk IP18 6JW (01502) 727222 **fax** (01502) 727223 **email** customerservices@adnams.co.uk **website** www.adnams.co.uk hours (Orderline) Mon–Fri 9–5.30
shops • Adnams Wine Shop, Pinkney's Lane, Southwold, Suffolk IP18 6EW Mon–Sat 9.30–5.30, Sun 10–4
• Adnams Cellar & Kitchen Store, 4 Drayman Square, Southwold, Suffolk IP18 6GB Mon–Sat 9–6, Sun 10–4
• Other shops in: Essex (Saffron Walden), Lincolnshire (Stamford), Norfolk (Harleston, Holt, Norwich, Wells-next-the-Sea), Suffolk (Hadleigh, Woodbridge), London (Spitalfields, Bloomsbury)
cards AmEx, Maestro, MasterCard, Visa, **delivery** Free for orders over £50 in most of mainland UK, otherwise £5.99 **en primeur** Bordeaux, Burgundy, Rhône. **G M T**
✪ *Historic and award-winning brewery also selling an extensive list of personality-packed wines from around the world, chosen by their enthusiastic team of buyers. There is also a new distillery at Southwold producing a range of spirits.*

Aldi Stores

head office Holly Lane, Atherstone, Warwickshire, CV9 2SQ; over 400 stores in the UK **customer service** 0844 406 8800; **website** www.aldi.co.uk
hours Mon–Fri 9–8, Sat 8.30–8, Sun 10–4 (selected stores; check website)
cards Maestro, Delta, Solo and Electron cards only. Visa and MasterCard credit cards accepted in Scottish stores and selected Welsh stores only.
✪ *Decent everyday stuff from around the world, with lots of wines under £4.*

armit

mail order/online 5 Royalty Studios, 105 Lancaster Road, London W11 1QF
(020) 7908 0600 **fax** (020) 7908 0601
email info@armit.co.uk **website** www.armit.co.uk **hours** Mon–Fri 8.45–5.15
cards Maestro, MasterCard, Visa **delivery** Free over £250, otherwise £15 delivery
charge **minimum order** 1 case; **en primeur** Bordeaux, Burgundy, Italy, Rhône,
New World. **C M T**
✪ *Top-quality wines from around the world, with a focus on Bordeaux, Burgundy and Italy.*
Particularly strong on wines to go with food – they supply some of the country's top restaurants.

ASDA

head office Asda House, Southbank, Great Wilson Street, Leeds LS11 5AD (0113) 243 5435
customer service (0800) 952 0101; 385 **stores** website www.asda.co.uk
hours Selected stores open 24 hours, see local store for details **cards** Maestro,
MasterCard, Visa.
✪ *Large and generally successful range of good-value wines at all price points, selected by*
Philippa Carr MW.

AustralianWineCentre.co.uk

mail order/online PO Box 3854, Datchet, Slough SL3 3EN 0800 756 1141 **fax** (01753) 208040
email customerservice@AustralianWineCentre.co.uk **website** www.AustralianWineCentre.
co.uk; **cards** MasterCard, Visa **delivery** Free for orders over £100, otherwise £5 per order;
UK mainland only **minimum order** 12 bottles.
✪ *The original Aussie specialist with some brilliant Australian wines.*

Averys Wine Merchants

head office 4 High Street, Nailsea, Bristol BS48 1BT 0843 224 1224
fax (01275) 811101 **email** enquiries@averys.com **website** www.averys.com
• Shop and Cellars, 9 Culver Street, Bristol BS1 5LD (0117) 921 4146 **fax** (0117) 922 6318
email cellars@averys.com **hours** Mon–Fri 8–8, Sat–Sun 9–6; Shop Mon–Sat 10–7
cards Maestro, MasterCard, Visa **delivery** £6.99 per delivery address **en primeur**
Bordeaux, Burgundy, Port, Rhône. **C G M T**
✪ *A small but very respectable selection from just about everywhere in France, Italy and Spain,*
as well as some good stuff from New Zealand, Australia and Chile.

Bancroft Wines

mail order Woolyard, 54 Bermondsey Street, London SE1 3UD (020) 7232 5440 **fax** (020)
7232 5451 **email** sales@bancroftwines.com **website** www.bancroftwines.com **hours** Mon–
Fri 9–5.30 **cards** Delta, Maestro, MasterCard, Visa **discounts** Negotiable **delivery** free for
London and mainland UK (minimum order 12 bottles); **en primeur** Bordeaux, Burgundy,
Rhône. **C M T**
✪ *Bancroft is UK agent for an impressive flotilla of French winemakers: from Burgundy, Rhône,*
Loire and southern France. There is also a fantastic selection of Italian, Spanish and New
World wines.

Barrica Wines

Huntley Gate Farm, Whalley Road, Samlesbury, Lancashire, PR5 0UN (01772) 877933
email wines@barricawines.co.uk **website** www.barricawines.co.uk **hours** Mon–Fri 10–6,
Sat & Bank Holidays 11–5; **cards** Maestro, MasterCard, Visa
delivery Free for local delivery, National courier delivery at cost;
minimum order 1 mixed case. **G M T**
✪ *Award-winning retailer in the Ribble Valley. Huge range of wines, beers and spirits.*

Bat & Bottle

Unit 5, 19 Pillings Road, Oakham LE15 6QF (01572) 759735
email ben@batwine.co.uk **website** www.batwine.co.uk **hours** Mon–Fri 10–4, Sat 9–2; ring
or check website before visiting **cards** Maestro, MasterCard, Visa
delivery Free for orders over £150. **G M T**
✪ *Ben and Emma Robson specialize in Italy, and in characterful wines from small producers.
They sell a few favourites from elsewhere, too.*

Bennetts Fine Wines

High Street, Chipping Campden, Glos GL55 6AG (01386) 840392 **fax** (01386) 840974
hours Mon–Sat 9.30–6 **email** william@bennettsfinewines.com
website www.bennettsfinewines.com **cards** Access, Maestro, MasterCard, Visa
discounts On collected orders of 1 case or more **delivery** £6 per case, minimum charge
£12, free for orders over £200 **en primeur** Burgundy, California, New Zealand, Rhône. **M**
• Edward Sheldon, New Street, Shipston-on-Stour, Warwickshire CV36 4EN (01608)
661409 fax (01608) 663166 **hours** Mon–Wed 9–6, Thur–Fri 9–7, Sat 9.30–5
✪ *Reasonable prices for high-calibre producers. Mainly from France and Italy, but some good
German, Spanish, Portuguese, Australian and New Zealand wines, too.*

Berkmann Wine Cellars

10–12 Brewery Road, London N7 9NH (020) 7609 4711 **fax** (020) 7607 0018
email orders@berkmann.co.uk **email** orders@pagendampratt.co.uk
website www.berkmann.co.uk **hours** Mon–Fri 9–5.30
cards Maestro, MasterCard, Visa **delivery** Free for orders over £150 to UK mainland
(excluding the Highlands) **minimum order** 1 mixed case **G M T**
• Brunel Park, Vincents Road, Bumpers Farm, Chippenham, Wiltshire SN14 6NQ (01249)
463501 **fax** (01249) 463502 **email** orders.chippenham@berkmann.co.uk
• Churchill Vintners, 401 Walsall Road, Perry Bar, Birmingham B42 1BT (0121) 356 8888
fax (0121) 356 1111 **email** sales@churchill-vintners.co.uk
• Pagendam Pratt Wine Cellars, 16 Marston Moor Business Park, Rudgate, Tockwith, North
Yorkshire YO26 7QF (01423) 357567 **fax** (01423) 357568
✪ *UK agent for many top wineries around the world. An incredibly diverse list, with some great
Italian wines.*

Berry Bros. & Rudd

3 St James's Street, London SW1A 1EG 0800 280 2440 **hours** Mon–Fri 10–6, Sat 10–5
sales and services 0800 280 2440 (lines open Mon–Fri 9–6, Sat 10–4) **fax** 0800 280 2443
email bbr@bbr.com **website** www.bbr.com **cards** AmEx, Diners, Maestro, MasterCard, Visa
delivery Free to most areas of the UK for orders of £100 or more **en primeur** Bordeaux,
Burgundy, Rhône. **C G M T**
• Berrys' Bin End Shop, Hamilton Close, Houndmills, Basingstoke, Hampshire RG21 6YB
0800 280 2440 **hours** Mon–Fri 10–6, Sat–Sun 10–4
✪ *Classy and wide-ranging list. There's an emphasis on the classic regions of France. Berry's
Own Selection is extensive, with wines made by world-class producers.*

Bibendum Wine

mail order 113 Regents Park Road, London NW1 8UR (020) 7449 4120 **fax** (020) 7449 4121
email sales@bibendum-wine.co.uk **website** www.bibendumfinewine.co.uk
hours Mon–Fri 9–5.30 **cards** Maestro, MasterCard, Visa **delivery** Free throughout
mainland UK for orders over £350, otherwise £15 **en primeur** Bordeaux, Burgundy, New
World, Rhône, Port. **M T**
✪ *Equally strong in the Old World and the New: St Cosme in the Rhône and Vietti in Piedmont
are matched by d'Arenberg and Katnook from Australia and Catena Zapata from Argentina.*

Big Red Wine Company

mail order Barton Coach House, The Street, Barton Mills, Suffolk IP28 6AA (01638) 510803
email sales@bigredwine.co.uk **website** www.bigredwine.co.uk **hours** Mon–Sat 9–6
cards AmEx, Delta, Maestro, MasterCard, Visa, PayPal
discounts 5–15% for Wine Club members; negotiable for large orders
delivery £7 per consignment for orders under £200, £10 for orders under £50, UK mainland
en primeur Bordeaux, Rhône, Southwest France. **C G M T**
✪ *Intelligently chosen, reliably individualistic wines from good estates in France, Italy
and Spain. A list worth reading, full of information and provocative opinion – and they're
not overcharging.*

Booths

central office Longridge Road, Ribbleton, Preston PR2 5BX (01772) 693800; 28 stores
across the North of England **fax** (01772) 693893 **website** www.booths.co.uk
hours Office: Mon–Fri 8.30–5; shop hours vary
cards AmEx, Electron, Maestro, MasterCard, Visa discounts 5% off any 6 bottles. **G T**
✪ *A list for any merchant to be proud of, never mind a supermarket. There's plenty around £5,
but if you're prepared to hand over £7–£9 you'll find some really interesting stuff.*

The following services are available where indicated: **C** = cellarage **G** = glass hire/loan **M** = mail/online order **T** = tastings and talks

163

Bordeaux Index

mail order/online 10 Hatton Garden, London EC1N 8AH (020) 7269 0700
fax (020) 7269 0701 **email** sales@bordeauxindex.com **website** www.bordeauxindex.com
hours Mon–Fri 8.30–6 **cards** AmEx, Maestro, MasterCard, Visa
delivery (Private sales only) free for orders over £2000 UK mainland; visit the website
for other delivery details, including international **minimum order** £100 or one unsplit case
of 12 **en primeur** Bordeaux, Burgundy, Rhône, Italy. **C M T**
✪ *Extensive list of fine wines, including older vintages, focused on the classic regions of France and Italy, but with interesting stuff from elsewhere.*

Budgens Stores

head office Musgrave House, Widewater Place, Moorhall Road, Harefield, Uxbridge,
Middlesex UB9 6NS 01895 828100 **fax** 0870 050 0159; 190 stores mainly in southern
England and East Anglia – for nearest store call 0800 298 0758
email customerservice@musgrave.co.uk **website** www.budgens.co.uk
hours Variable; usually Mon–Sat 8–8, Sun 10–4 **cards** Maestro, MasterCard, Visa.
✪ *These days you can be reasonably confident of going into Budgens and coming out with something you'd really like to drink.*

The Butlers Wine Cellar

247 Queens Park Road, Brighton BN2 9XJ (01273) 698724
email henry@butlers-winecellar.co.uk
website www.butlers-winecellar.co.uk **hours** Mon–Wed, Fri 11–7, Thur, Sat 11–8, Sun 12–6
cards Access, AmEx, Maestro, MasterCard, Visa delivery Free nationally over £150
en primeur Bordeaux. **G M T**
• 88 St George's Road, Kemptown, Brighton BN2 1EE (01273) 621638
hours Tues–Sat 12–8pm
✪ *Henry Butler personally chooses the wines and there is some fascinating stuff here, including English wines from local growers such as Breaky Bottom and Ridgeview. Check the website or join the mailing list as offers change regularly.*

Anthony Byrne Fine Wines

mail order Ramsey Business Park, Stocking Fen Road, Ramsey, Cambs PE26 2UR
(01487) 814555 **fax** (01487) 814962 **email** anthony@abfw.co.uk or gary@abfw.co.uk
website www.abfw.co.uk **hours** Mon–Fri 9–5.30 **cards** MasterCard, Visa
discounts Available on cases **delivery** Free 5 cases or more, or orders of £250 or more;
otherwise £15 **minimum order** 1 case **en primeur** Bordeaux, Burgundy, Rhône. **C M T**
✪ *A serious range of Burgundy; smaller but focused lists from Bordeaux and the Rhône; carefully selected wines from Alsace, Loire and Provence; and a wide range of New World.*

D Byrne & Co

Victoria Buildings, 12 King Street, Clitheroe, Lancashire BB7 2EP (01200) 423152
website www.dbyrne-finewines.co.uk **hours** Mon–Wed, Sat 8.30–6, Thur–Fri 8.30–8
cards Maestro, MasterCard, Visa **delivery** Free within 30 miles; nationally £10 1st case,
further cases additional £2.50 **en primeur** Bordeaux, Burgundy, Rhône, Germany. **G M T**

✪ *A family business since the 1870s and one of northern England's best wine merchants. A hugely impressive range of wines, as well as over 300 malt whiskies and over 30 vodkas. I urge you to go and see for yourself.*

Cambridge Wine Merchants

head office 29 Dry Drayton Industries, Scotland Road, Dry Drayton CB23 8AT (01954) 214528 **fax** (01954) 214574 **email** cambridgewine@cambridgewine.com **website** www.cambridgewine.com **hours** Mon–Sat 10am–9pm, Sun 12–8 **cards** Amex, MasterCard, Switch, Visa **discounts** Buy 4 bottles, get the cheapest one free (selected lines) **delivery** Free for 12 bottles or more within 5 miles of Cambridge; £2.50 for less than 12 bottles. National delivery £7.50 per case of 12 bottles; £9.99 for 1 to 11 bottles **en primeur** Bordeaux, Burgundy, Rhône, Port. **C G M T**
• 42 Mill Road, Cambridge CB1 2AD (01223) 568993 **email** mill@cambridgewine.com
• 32 Bridge Street, Cambridge CB2 1UJ (01223) 568989 **email** bridge@cambridgewine.com
• 2 King's Parade, Cambridge CB2 1SJ (01223) 309309 **email** kings@cambridgewine.com
• 163 Cherry Hinton Road, Cambridge CB1 7BX (01223) 214548 **email** cherry@cambridgewine.com
• 12 Church Street, Ampthill MK45 2PL (01525) 405929 **email** ampthill@cambridgewine.com
• 34b Kneesworth Street, Royston SG8 5AB (01763) 247076 **email** royston@cambridgewine.com
• 5 Winchester Street, Salisbury SP1 1HB (01722) 324486 **email** salisbury@cambridgewine.com
• Edinburgh Wine Merchants, 30b Raeburn Place, Edinburgh EH4 IHN (0131) 343 2347 **email** stockbridge@edinburghwine.com
✪ *Young, unstuffy merchants with a well-chosen list: good, individual producers, with particularly interesting Australian, German, Champagne. Port and dessert sections. Every branch has a wine-tasting club.*

Les Caves de Pyrène

Pew Corner, Old Portsmouth Road, Artington, Guildford GU3 1LP (office) (01483) 538820 (shop) (01483) 554750 **fax** (01483) 455068 **email** sales@lescaves.co.uk **website** www.lescaves.co.uk **hours** Wed–Fri 9–5 **cards** Maestro, MasterCard, Visa **delivery** Free for orders over £200 within London, elsewhere at cost **G M T**
✪ *Excellent operation; devotees of 'natural wines'. France and Italy are particularly strong and there's some choice stuff from Spain, Australia and New Zealand.*

Cockburns of Leith

mail order/online Thistle House, Caputhall Road, Deans Industrial Estate, Livingston EH54 8AS (01506) 468 900 **fax** (01506) 414 486 **email** imacphail-cockburns@wine-importers.net **website** www.cockburnsofleith.co.uk **hours** Mon–Fri 9–5 **cards** Maestro, MasterCard, Visa **delivery** Free 12 or more bottles within Edinburgh; elsewhere £9.99 **en primeur** Bordeaux, Burgundy. **M**
✪ *Scotland's oldest surviving wine merchant, founded in 1796; under new ownership since 2010. Most major wine regions covered. Older vintages of Bordeaux, Burgundy and the Rhône.*

Connolly's Wine Merchants

Arch 13, 220 Livery Street, Birmingham B3 1EU (0121) 236 3837/9269 **fax** (0121) 233 2339
hours Mon–Fri 10–6.30, Sat 10-4 **website** www.connollyswine.co.uk **cards** AmEx, Maestro,
MasterCard, Visa **delivery** National delivery available (charges apply) **discounts** 10% for
12 or more bottles **en primeur** Burgundy. **G M T**
• 379-381 Warwick Road, Olton, Solihull, B91 1BQ (0121) 709 3734/ (0121) 236 9269
hours Mon-Wed 10-8, Thurs-Fri 10-9, Sat 10-8, Sun 11-5
✪ *Award-winning merchant that has something for everyone. Burgundy, Bordeaux and the
Rhône all look very good; and there are top names from Germany, Italy, Spain and California.
Weekly in-store tastings, monthly tutored tastings and winemaker dinners. Birmingham's
largest whisky retailer, too.*

The Co-operative Group

head office New Century House, Manchester M60 4ES Freephone 0800 0686 727 for stock
details; over 2800 licensed stores **email** customer.relations@co-operative.coop
website www.co-operative.coop **hours** Variable **cards** Variable.
✪ *Champions of Fairtrade. The Co-op is stocking some good wine at the moment, most of it
under £10. A small list of fine wines between £10 and £20 available in premium stores.*

Corney & Barrow

head office No. 1 Thomas More Street, London E1W 1YZ (020) 7265 2400
fax (020) 7265 2444 **hours** Mon–Fri 8–6 (24-hr answering machine)
email wine@corneyandbarrow.com **website** www.corneyandbarrow.com
hours Mon–Fri 9–6 **cards** AmEx, Maestro, MasterCard, Visa **delivery** Free for all orders
above £200 within mainland UK, otherwise £12.50 per delivery. **en primeur** Bordeaux,
Burgundy, Champagne, Rhône, Italy, Spain. **C G M T**
• Corney & Barrow East Anglia, Belvoir House, High Street, Newmarket CB8 8DH
(01638) 600000 **hours** Mon–Sat 9–6
• Corney & Barrow (Scotland) with Whighams of Ayr, 8 Academy Street, Ayr KA7 1HT
(01292) 267000 **hours** Mon–Sat 10–5.30
• Oxenfoord Castle, by Pathhead, Midlothian EH37 5UB (01875) 321921
✪ *Top names in French and other European wines; Australia, South Africa and South America
are also impressive. Wines in every price bracket – try them out at Corney & Barrow wine bars
in London.*

Dalling & Co

mail order 22 High Street, Kings Langley, Herts, WD4 8BH 01923 262083
hours Mon–Wed 9:30–7, Thurs-Sat 9 -9 **email** jeff@dallingandco.com or
mark@dallingandco.com **website** www.dallingandco.com
cards AmEx, Maestro, MasterCard, Visa **discounts** 5% for unmixed dozens.
delivery Free for local orders; UK shipping available **G M T**
✪ *Lucky old Kings Langley to have this relatively new (2009) delicatessen and wine merchant
on the doorstep. They sell a wide range of wines, spirits, beers and ales and everything from
hampers to Cuban cigars. They even stock a new favourite of mine, Coates & Seely Méthode
Britannique rosé, a sparkling rosé from the chalk downlands of Hampshire.*

DeFINE Food & Wine

Chester Road, Sandiway, Cheshire CW8 2NH (01606) 882101 **fax** (01606) 888407
email office@definefoodandwine.com **website** www.definefoodandwine.com
hours Mon–Sat 10–7, Sun 11–2 **cards** AmEx, Maestro, MasterCard, Visa
discounts 5% off 12 bottles or more **delivery** Free locally, otherwise £7.50 UK. **C G M T**
✪ *Wine shop and delicatessen, with British cheeses and many food specialities from Italy and Spain. Excellent, wide-ranging list of over 1000 wines including a strong line-up from Argentina, New Zealand and South Africa, as well as European classics.*

Devigne Wines

mail order PO Box 13748, North Berwick EH39 9AA (01620) 890860 **fax** (05600) 756 287
email info@devignewines.co.uk **website** www.devignewines.co.uk **hours** Mon–Fri
10–6 **cards** AmEx, Maestro, MasterCard, Visa, PayPal **discounts** Selected mixed cases
at introductory rate **delivery** Free for orders over £50, otherwise £6.85 per consignment;
please ring for quote for Highlands and Islands. **M**
✪ *Small list specializing in French wine: traditional-method sparkling wines from all over France; a wide choice of rosés; Gaillac from the Southwest; and wines from the Languedoc and the Arbois in the Jura.*

Direct Wine See Laithwaite's.

Direct Wine Shipments

5–7 Corporation Square, Belfast, Northern Ireland BT1 3AJ (028) 9050 8000
fax (028) 9050 8002 **email** shop@directwine.co.uk and info@directwine.co.uk
website www.directwine.co.uk **hours** Mon–Fri 9.30–7 (Thur 10–8), Sat 9.30–5.30
cards Delta, Electron, Maestro, MasterCard, Solo, Switch, Visa **discounts** 10% in the form
of complimentary wine with each case **delivery** Free Northern Ireland 1 case or more,
variable delivery charge for UK mainland depending on customer spend.
en primeur Bordeaux, Burgundy, Rhône. **C M T**
✪ *Rhône, Spain, Australia and Burgundy outstanding; Italy, Germany and Chile not far behind; there's good stuff from pretty much everywhere. Also wine courses, tastings and expert advice.*

Nick Dobson Wines

mail order 3 The Grove, Idle, West Yorkshire 0800 849 3078 **fax** 0870 460 2358
email nick.dobson@nickdobsonwines.co.uk **website** www.nickdobsonwines.co.uk
hours Mon–Fri 9–5 **cards** Access, Maestro, MasterCard, Visa **delivery** £8.95 + VAT
1 case; £7.95 + VAT 2nd and subsequent cases to UK mainland addresses. **M T**
✪ *Specialist in wines from Switzerland, Austria and Beaujolais, plus intriguing selections from elsewhere in Europe and Israel.*

Domaine Direct

mail order 6–9 Cynthia Street, London N1 9JF (020) 7837 1142 **fax** (020) 7837 8605
email mail@domainedirect.co.uk **website** www.domainedirect.co.uk
hours Mon–Fri 8.30–6 or answering machine **cards** Maestro, MasterCard, Visa
delivery Free London; elsewhere in UK mainland 1 case £15, 2 cases £21.00, 3 cases £24,

4 or more free and for all orders over £430 + VAT. **minimum order** 1 mixed case
en primeur Burgundy (in top vintages). **C M T**
✪ *Sensational Burgundy list; prices are very reasonable for the quality. Also a full range from Western Australia star Leeuwin Estate.*

Farr Vintners

mail order/online only 220 Queenstown Road, Battersea, London SW8 4LP (020) 7821 2000
fax (020) 7821 2020 **email** sales@farrvintners.com **website** www.farrvintners.com
hours Mon–Fri 9–6 **cards** Access, Maestro, MasterCard, Visa **delivery** London £1 per case
(min £15); elsewhere at cost **minimum order** £500 + VAT **en primeur** Bordeaux. **C M T**
✪ *One of the UK's largest stockholders of top Bordeaux wines and leading* en primeur
merchant. They have a fantastic list of the world's finest wines. As well as Bordeaux, you'll also find top stuff and older vintages of white Burgundy, red Rhône, plus Italy, Australia and California, as well as vintage Port and Madeira.

Fingal-Rock

64 Monnow Street, Monmouth NP25 3EN **tel & fax** 01600 712372
email tom@pinotnoir.co.uk **website** www.pinotnoir.co.uk **hours** Mon 9.30–1.30, Thur & Fri
9.30–5.30, Sat 9.30–5 **cards** Maestro, MasterCard, Visa **discounts** 5% for at least 12 bottles
collected from shop, 7.5% for collected orders over £500, 10% for collected orders over
£1200 **delivery** Free locally (within 30 miles); orders further afield free if over £100. **G M T**
✪ *The website address gives you a clue that the list's great strength is Burgundy, especially reds. There are wines from some very good growers and at a range of prices between £8 and £40. Small but tempting selections from other French regions, as well as other parts of Europe and the New World and wines from local producer, Monnow Valley. Definitely worth a visit if you are in the area.*

Flagship Wines

417 Hatfield Road, St Albans, Hertfordshire AL4 0XP (01727) 865309
email sales@flagshipwines.co.uk **website** www.flagshipwines.co.uk
hours Tues–Thur 11–6, Fri 11–7.30, Sat 10–6 **cards** Maestro, MasterCard, Visa
delivery Free to St Albans addresses and £10 to other UK mainland addresses. **G M T**
✪ *Independent whose prices can match those of the supermarkets – plus friendly, well-informed advice from boss Julia Jenkins. Strong in Australia, New Zealand, Argentina, France and Spain but great stuff all round. Programme of tastings and events.*

Fortnum & Mason

181 Piccadilly, London W1A 1ER (020) 7734 8040 **fax** (020) 7437 3278 **ordering line**
(020) 7973 4136 **email** info@fortnumandmason.co.uk **website** www.fortnumandmason.
com **hours** Mon–Sat 10–8, Sun 12–6 (Food Hall and Patio Restaurant only)
cards AmEx, Diners, Maestro, MasterCard, Visa **discounts** 1 free bottle per unmixed
dozen **delivery** £4.95 per delivery address **en primeur** Bordeaux. **M T**
✪ *Impressive names from just about everywhere, including Champagne, Bordeaux, Burgundy, Italy, Germany, Australia, New Zealand, South Africa and California. Impeccably sourced own-label range.*

Friarwood

26 New King's Road, London SW6 4ST (020) 7736 2628 **fax** (020) 7731 0411
email simon.mckay@friarwood.com **website** www.friarwood.com
hours Mon–Sat 10–7 **cards** AmEx, Maestro, MasterCard, Visa, Solo, Electron
discounts 5% on cases of 12 (mixed and unmixed) **delivery** Locally free of charge, orders
for the mainland over £200 free, not including Highlands and Islands. Highlands and
Islands delivery will be quoted with order. **en primeur** Bordeaux. **C G M T**
✪ *The focus is Bordeaux, including mature wines from a good selection of* petits châteaux *as
well as classed growths. Burgundy and other French regions are strong, too.*

FromVineyardsDirect.com

online only Northburgh House, 10 Northburgh Street, London EC1V 0AT
(020) 7549 7900 **fax** (020) 7253 9539 **email** info@fromvineyardsdirect.com
website www.fromvineyardsdirect.com **hours** 9–6 **cards** Maestro, MasterCard, Visa, Solo,
Switch **delivery** Free **minimum order** 1 case (12 bottles) in UK mainland; 2 cases
in Northern Ireland, Scottish Highlands and islands **en primeur** Bordeaux. **C M T**
✪ *A hand-picked selection of wines direct from vineyards in France, Italy and Spain, at very
affordable prices.*

Gauntleys of Nottingham

4 High Street, Exchange Arcade, Nottingham NG1 2ET (0115) 911 0555 **fax** (0115) 911 0557
email rhône@gauntleywine.com **website** www.gauntleys.com **hours** Mon–Sat
9–5.30 **cards** AmEx, Maestro, MasterCard, Visa **delivery** 1 case £11.95, 2–3 cases £9.95,
4 or more cases free **en primeur** Alsace, Burgundy, Loire, Rhône, southern France,
Spain. **M T**
✪ *Award-winning Rhône and Alsace lists. Loire, Burgundy, southern France and Spain are also
excellent.*

Goedhuis & Co

6 Rudolf Place, Miles Street, London SW8 1RP (020) 7793 7900 **fax** (020) 7793 7170
email sales@goedhuis.com **website** www.goedhuis.com **hours** Mon–Fri 9–5.30
cards Maestro, MasterCard, Visa **delivery** Free on orders over £250 ex-VAT; otherwise £15
ex-VAT England, elsewhere at cost **minimum order** 1 unmixed case **en primeur** Bordeaux,
Burgundy, Rhône. **C G M T**
✪ *Fine wine specialist. Bordeaux, Burgundy and the Rhône are the core of the list, but
everything is good. A sprinkling of New World producers, too.*

retailers' directory

The following services are available where indicated: **C** = cellarage **G** = glass hire/loan **M** = mail/online order **T** = tastings and talks

169

Great Western Wine

Wells Road, Bath BA2 3AP (01225) 322810 (enquiries and orders) fax (01225) 427231
email wine@greatwesternwine.co.uk **website** www.greatwesternwine.co.uk
hours Mon–Fri 10–7, Sat 10–6 **cards** AmEx, Maestro, MasterCard, Visa **discounts** Wine –
5% off mixed dozen, 10% off unsplit dozen. Sparkling wine –10% off 6 bottles, 20% off
12 bottles **delivery** Free for 12 bottles or more in UK mainland; £5.95 for 1–3 bottles,
£8.95 for 4–11 bottles **en primeur** Australia, Bordeaux, Burgundy, Rhône. **C G M T**
✪ *Wide-ranging list, bringing in brilliant wines from individual growers around the world, from
Argentina to the USA, via Israel, Morocco and Uruguay. Also organizes events and tastings.*

Peter Green & Co

37A/B Warrender Park Road, Edinburgh EH9 1HJ (0131) 229 5925
email shop@petergreenwines.com **website** www.petergreenwines.co.uk
hours Tues–Thur 10–6.30, Fri 10–7.30, Sat 10–6.30 **cards** Maestro, MasterCard,
Visa **delivery** Free in Edinburgh **minimum order** (For delivery) 1 case. **G T**
✪ *Extensive and adventurous list: Tunisia, India and the Lebanon rub shoulders with the more
classic wine countries.*

Green & Blue

36–38 Lordship Lane, East Dulwich, London SE22 8HJ (020) 8693 9250
email info@greenandbluewines.com **website** www.greenandbluewines.com
hours Mon–Wed 9–11, Thur–Sat 9–midnight, Sun 11–5 **cards** Delta, Maestro, MasterCard,
Visa **discounts** 5% off mixed cases of 12 (collection only), 10% on unmixed cases
delivery Free within 2 miles for over £200, otherwise £10 per delivery within M25; £10 per
case outside M25. **T**
✪ *A tempting list full of unusual wines you really want to drink, many of them from small
producers – and you can try them on the spot in the friendly wine bar, which serves tapas-style
food. The staff are knowledgeable, and there's a waiting list for the tutored tastings in Green &
Blue's School of Wine. Monthly wine dinners are popular, too.*

Halifax Wine Company

18 Prescott Street, Halifax, West Yorkshire HX1 2LG (01422) 256333
email andy@halifaxwinecompany.com **website** www.halifaxwinecompany.com
hours Tues–Thur 9–5, Fri 9–6, Sat 9–5. Closed first week in January and first week in
August **cards** Access, Maestro, MasterCard, Visa **discounts** 8% on 12 bottles or more (can
be unsplit cases) for personal callers to the shop **delivery** Free to HX postcodes on orders
over £85; rest of UK mainland – delivery charges apply depending on order value. **M T**
✪ *Exciting, wide-ranging and award-winning list, and at keen prices, too. Portugal (fantastic list
of Madeiras going back to Blandy's Sercial 1910), Spain and Italy are the strong points but there
is plenty from the New World, too.*

Handford Wines

105 Old Brompton Road, South Kensington, London SW7 3LE (020) 7589 6113
fax (020) 7581 2983 **email** mick@handford.net **website** www.handford.net **hours** Mon–Sat
10–8.30, Sun 11–5 **cards** AmEx, Maestro, MasterCard, Visa **discounts** 5% on mixed cases

delivery £10 for orders under £150 within UK **en primeur** Bordeaux, Burgundy, Rhône, Port. **C G M T**

✪ *Delightful London shop absolutely packed with the sort of wines I really want to drink.Over 1500 wines to choose from.*

hangingditch wine merchants
Britannic Buildings, 42–44 Victoria Street, Manchester M3 1ST (0161) 832 8222
email wine@hangingditch.com **website** www.hangingditch.com **hours** Mon–Wed 10–6, Thur–Sat 10–8, Sun 1–5 **cards** AmEx, MasterCard, Visa, all debit cards **discounts** 5% on 6–11 bottles, 10% on 12 bottles or more **delivery** Free for cases within 10 miles; national deliveries: £7.50 for up to 12 bottles **G M T**

✪ *Primarily a wine merchant but also promotes the 'vinoteca' concept – wines by the glass available from a rotating selection or by the bottle for retail price plus a fixed £6 corkage. Food and wine matching and bespoke tasting events and gourmet dinners also on offer.*

Harvey Nichols
109–125 Knightsbridge, London SW1X 7RJ (020) 7235 5000 **hours** Mon–Sat 10–8, Sun 12–6
website www.harveynichols.com **cards** AmEx, Maestro, MasterCard, Visa. **M T**
• The Mailbox, 31–32 Wharfside Street, Birmingham B1 1RE (0121) 616 6024
hours Mon–Sat 10–7, Sun 11–5
• 107–111 Briggate, Leeds LS1 6AZ (0113) 204 8888 **hours** Mon–Wed 10–6, Thur 10–8, Fri–Sat 10–7, Sun 11–5
• 21 New Cathedral Street, Manchester M1 1AD (0161) 828 8888 **hours** Mon–Fri 10–8, Sat 9–7, Sun 11–5
• 27 Philadelphia Street, Quakers Friars, Cabot Circus, Bristol BS1 3BZ
(0117) 916 8888 **hours** Mon–Wed 10––6, Thur 10–8, Fri–Sat 10–7, Sun 11–5
• 30–34 St Andrew Square, Edinburgh EH2 2AD (0131) 524 8322 **hours** Mon–Wed 10–6, Thur 10–8, Fri, Sat 10–7, Sun 11–6
• Dundrum Town Centre, Sandyford Road, Dublin 16, +353 (0) 1291 0420 **hours** Mon–Tues 10–7, Wed–Fri 10–9, Sat 10–7, Sun 11–7

✪ *Sought-after producers and cult fine wines, especially from France (plenty of smart Champagne here), Italy and California.*

Haynes Hanson & Clark
Sheep Street, Stow-on-the-Wold, Gloucestershire GL54 1AA (01451) 870808
fax (01451) 870508 **hours** Mon–Fri 9–6, Sat 9–5.30
• 7 Elystan Street, London SW3 3NT (020) 7584 7927 **fax** (020) 7584 7967
hours Mon–Fri 9–7, Sat 9–4.30 **email** stow@hhandc.co.uk or london@hhandc.co.uk
website www.hhandc.co.uk **cards** Maestro, MasterCard, Switch, Visa **discounts** 10% unsplit case **delivery** Free for 1 case or more in central London and areas covered by Stow-on-the-Wold van; elsewhere 1 case £15.60, 2–3 cases £9.75 per case, 4 or more cases £8.10 per case, free on orders over £650 **en primeur** Bordeaux, Burgundy. **M T**

✪ *Known for its subtle, elegant wines: top-notch Burgundy is the main focus of the list, but other French regions are well represented, and there's interesting stuff from Spain, Italy, Australia and New Zealand. Good house Champagne.*

Hedley Wright

The Hitchin (Wyevale) Centre, Cambridge Road, Hitchin, Hertfordshire SG4 0JT
(01462) 431110 **fax** (01462) 422983 **hours** Tues–Fri 11–7, Sat 10–7, Sun 11–5
email sales@hedleywright.co.uk **website** www.hedleywright.co.uk
cards AmEx, Maestro, MasterCard, Visa **delivery** £5 per delivery, free for orders over
£100 **minimum order** 1 bottle
✪ *A good all-round list, especially strong in Australia, France, Italy, Spain and South Africa.*

Hicks & Don

17 Kingsmead Business Park, Shaftesbury Road, Gillingham, Dorset SP8 5FB
(01747) 824292 **fax** (01747) 826963 **email** mailbox@hicksanddon.co.uk
website www.hicksanddon.co.uk **hours** Mon–Fri 9–6 **cards** Maestro, MasterCard,
Visa **discounts** Negotiable **delivery** Free over £100, otherwise £8 per case in UK
mainland **minimum order** 1 case **en primeur** Bordeaux, Burgundy, Chablis, Chile, Italy,
Port, Rhône, Beaujolais, Alace, Australia and New Zealand. **C G M T**
✪ *Subtle, well-made wines that go with food, particularly French wines. Still plenty of choice*
under £10.

Jeroboams (incorporating Laytons)

head office 7–9 Elliot's Place, London N1 8HX (020) 7288 8888 **fax** (020) 7359 2616
hours Mon–Fri 9–5.30 **shop** 50–52 Elizabeth Street, London SW1W 9PB (020) 7730 8108
email sales@jeroboams.co.uk **website** www.jeroboams.co.uk **hours shops** Mon–Sat
9.30/10–7 (may vary) **cards** AmEx, Maestro, MasterCard, Visa **delivery** Free for orders over
£250, otherwise £17.25 **en primeur** Bordeaux, Burgundy, Rhône. **C G M T**
• 20 Davies Street, London W1K 3DT (020) 7499 1015
• 13 Elgin Crescent, London W11 2JA (020) 7229 0527
• 29 Heath Street, London NW3 6TR (020) 7435 6845
• 96 Holland Park Avenue, London W11 3RB (020) 7727 9359
• 6 Pont Street, London SW1X 9EL (020) 7235 1612
• 1 St John's Wood High Street, London NW8 7NG (020) 7722 4020
• 56 Walton Street, London SW3 1RB (020) 7589 2020
• Mr Christian's Delicatessen, 11 Elgin Crescent, London W11 2JA (020) 7229 0501
• Milroy's of Soho, 3 Greek Street, London W1D 4NX (020) 7437 2385 (whisky and wine)
✪ *Wide-ranging list of affordable and enjoyable wines, especially good in France, Italy, Australia*
and New Zealand. Fine foods, especially cheeses and olive oils, are available in the Holland Park
and Mr Christian's Delicatessen shops.

S H Jones

27 High Street, Banbury, Oxfordshire OX16 5EW (01295) 251179 **fax** (01295) 272352
email banbury@shjones.com **website** www.shjones.com **hours** Mon–Sat 9.30-5.30
cards Maestro, MasterCard, Visa **delivery** Free for 12 bottles of wine/spirits or total value
over £100 within 30-mile radius of shops, otherwise £9.75 per case
en primeur Burgundy, Port, New Zealand, South Africa, Australia, Italy, Spain. **G M T**
• 9 Market Square, Bicester, Oxfordshire OX26 6AA (01869) 322448
email bicester@shjones.com

• The Cellar Shop, 2 Riverside, Tramway Road, Banbury, Oxfordshire OX16 5TU (01295) 672296 **fax** (01295) 259560 **email** retail@shjones.com
• 121 Regent Street, Leamington Spa, Warwickshire CV32 4NU (01926) 315609 **email** leamington@shjones.com
✪ *Wide-ranging list with good stuff from France, Italy and Spain, exciting New World selection, and plenty of tasty wine for less than £10.*

Justerini & Brooks
mail order 61 St James's Street, London SW1A 1LZ (020) 7484 6400 **fax** (020) 7484 6455 **email** justorders@justerinis.com **website** www.justerinis.com **hours** Mon–Fri 9–5.30 **cards** Maestro, MasterCard, Visa **delivery** Free for unmixed cases over £250, otherwise £15 + VAT in UK mainland **minimum order** 1 case **en primeur** Alsace, Bordeaux, Burgundy, Italy, Spain, Loire, Rhône, Germany. **C M T**
✪ *Superb list of top-quality wines from Europe's classic regions, as well as some excellent New World choices.*

Laithwaites Wine
mail order New Aquitaine House, Exeter Way, Theale, Reading, Berkshire RG7 4PL **order line** 0845 194 7720 **fax** 0845 194 7766 **email** customerservices@laithwaites.co.uk **website** www.laithwaites.co.uk **hours** Mon–Fri 8.30–9, Sat 9–8, Sun 9–6 **cards** AmEx, Diners, Maestro, MasterCard, Visa **discounts** On unmixed cases of 6 or 12 **delivery** £7.99 per delivery address **minimum order** No minimum order but most offers available in 6 or 12 bottle cases (mixed and unmixed) **en primeur** Australia, Bordeaux, Burgundy, Rhône, Rioja. **C M T**
• Flagship store: The Arch, 219–221 Stoney Street, London SE1 9AA (020) 7407 6378 **fax** (020) 7407 5411 **email** thearch@laithwaiteswine.com **hours** Mon–Thur 10–7, Fri 10–10, Sat 10–8, Sun 12–6
✪ *Mail order specialist with new flagship store just off Borough Market and 10 other shops in the Southeast and the Midlands. Extensive selection of wines from France, Australia, Spain, Italy and elsewhere.*

Lay & Wheeler
mail order Holton Park, Holton St Mary, Suffolk CO7 6NN (01473) 313300 **fax** (01473) 313264 **email** sales@laywheeler.com **website** www.laywheeler.com **hours** (Order office) Mon–Fri 8.30–5.30 **cards** AmEx, Maestro, MasterCard, Visa **delivery** £9.95; free for orders over £200 **en primeur** Bordeaux, Burgundy, Port (some vintages), Rhône, Spain, Portugal, Germany, Austria, Champagne. **C M T**
✪ *A must-have list with first-class Bordeaux and Burgundy to satisfy the most demanding drinker, and plenty more besides. En primeur and fine wines are two core strengths here.*

Lea & Sandeman
170 Fulham Road, London SW10 9PR (020) 7244 0522 **fax** (020) 7244 0533 **email** info@leaandsandeman.co.uk **website** www.leaandsandeman.co.uk **hours** Mon–Sat 10–8 **cards** AmEx, Maestro, MasterCard, Visa **discounts** 5–15% by the case, other discounts on 10 cases or more **delivery** London £10 for less than £100,

otherwise all orders over £100 free to UK mainland south of Perth. **en primeur** Bordeaux, Burgundy, Italy. **C G M T**
• 51 High Street, Barnes, London SW13 9LN (020) 8878 8643
• 211 Kensington Church Street, London W8 7LX (020) 7221 1982
• 167 Chiswick High Road, London W4 2DR (020) 8995 7355
✪ *Burgundy and Italy take precedence here, and there's a succession of excellent names, chosen with great care by Charles Lea and Patrick Sandeman. Bordeaux has wines at all prices, and there are short but fascinating ranges from the USA, Spain, Australia and New Zealand.*

Liberty Wines
mail order Unit D18, The Food Market, New Covent Garden, London SW8 5LL
(020) 7720 5350 **fax** (020) 7720 6158 **email** order@libertywines.co.uk
website www.libertywines.co.uk **hours** Mon–Fri 9–5.30 **cards** Maestro, MasterCard, Visa **delivery** Free to mainland UK **minimum order** 12 x 75cl bottles. **M**
✪ *Italy rules, with superb wines from pretty well all the best producers. Liberty is the UK agent for most of its producers, so if you're interested in Italian wines this should be your first port of call. Also top names from Australia, Argentina, USA and elsewhere. There's even icewine from Canada.*

Linlithgow Wines
Crossford, Station Road, Linlithgow, West Lothian EH49 6BW (01506) 848821
email linlithgowwines@aol.co.uk **website** www.linlithgowwines.co.uk **hours** Flexible (please phone first) **cards** None: cash, cheque or bank transfer only **delivery** £5 locally; elsewhere in UK £9 for 1 case, £15 for 2 cases and £5 per case thereafter. **G M T**
✪ *Terrific list of French wines, many imported direct from family-run vineyards in southern France.*

O W Loeb & Co
mail order 3 Archie Street, off Tanner Street, London SE1 3JT (020) 7234 0385
fax (020) 7357 0440 **email** finewine@owloeb.com **website** www.owloeb.com
hours Mon–Fri 8.30–5.30 **cards** Maestro, MasterCard, Visa **discounts** 24 bottles and above **delivery** Free for 24 bottles and above except north of Glasgow and Edinburgh **minimum order** 12 bottles **en primeur** Burgundy, Bordeaux, Rhône, Germany (Mosel). **C M T**
✪ *Burgundy, the Rhône, Loire and Germany stand out, with top producers galore. Then there are Loeb's new discoveries from Spain and the New World, especially New Zealand and South Africa.*

Majestic (see also Wine and Beer World)
head office Majestic House, Otterspool Way, Watford, Herts WD25 8WW (01923) 298200
fax (01923) 819105; 181 stores nationwide **email** info@majestic.co.uk
website www.majestic.co.uk **hours** Mon–Fri 10–8, Sat 9–7, Sun 10–5 (may vary)
cards AmEx, Diners, Maestro, MasterCard, Visa **delivery** Free UK mainland if you buy 12 or more bottles **minimum order** (in-store) 1 mixed case (6 bottles)
en primeur Bordeaux, Port, Burgundy. **G M T**

✪ *One of the best places to buy Champagne, with a good range and good discounts for buying in quantity. Loads of interesting and reasonably priced stuff, especially from France, Germany and the New World.*

Marks & Spencer
head office Waterside House, 35 North Wharf Road, London W2 1NW (020) 7935 4422 **fax** (020) 7487 2679; 600 licensed stores **website** www.marksandspencer.com **hours** Variable **discounts** Variable, a selection of 10 different Wines of the Month, buy any 6 and save 10% in selected stores. **M T**
✪ *M&S works with top producers around the world to create its impressive list of own-label wines. All the wines are exclusive and unique to M&S, selected by the company's in-house winemaking team.*

Martinez Wines
35 The Grove, Ilkley, Leeds, West Yorkshire LS29 9NJ (01943) 600000 **fax** 0870 922 3940 **email** shop¬@martinez.co.uk **website** www.martinez.co.uk **hours** Mon–Wed 10–6, Thur–Fri 10–8, Sat 9.30–6 Sun 12–6 **cards** AmEx, Maestro, MasterCard, Visa **discounts** 5% on 6 bottles or more, 10% on orders over £150 **delivery** Free local delivery, otherwise £6.99 per case mainland UK **en primeur** Bordeaux, Burgundy. **C G M T**
✪ *From a wide-ranging list, I'd single out the selections from France, Italy, Spain, Australia, Argentina and South Africa.*

Millésima
mail order 87 Quai de Paludate, CS 11691, 33050 Bordeaux Cedex, France (00 33) 5 57 80 88 08 **fax** (00 33) 5 57 80 88 19 **website** www.millesima.com **hours** Mon–Fri 8–5.30 **cards** AmEx, Diners, Maestro, MasterCard, Visa **delivery** For bottled wines, free to single UK addresses for orders exceeding £500. Otherwise, a charge of £20 will be applied. For en primeur wines, free to single UK addresses.**en primeur** Bordeaux, Burgundy, Champagne, Alsace, Rhône. **M T**
✪ *Wine comes direct from the châteaux to Millésima's 200-year-old cellars, where 2.5 million bottles are stored. Bordeaux and Burgundy are the core strengths, with vintages going back to the 1980s and including a large selection of magnums, double magnums, jeroboams (5 litres) and imperiales (6 litres). Plus a sprinkling of established names from Burgundy, Alsace, the Rhône and Champagne.*

Montrachet
mail order 11 Catherine Place, London SW1E 6DX (020) 7821 1337 **email** charles@montrachetwine.com **website** www.montrachetwine.com **hours** Mon–Fri 8.30–5.30 **cards** AmEx, Maestro, MasterCard, Visa **delivery** England and Wales £15, free for 3 or more cases; for Scotland ring for details **minimum order** 1 unmixed case **en primeur** Bordeaux, Burgundy. **C M T**
✪ *Impressive Burgundies are the main attraction here, but there are also some very good Rhônes, and Bordeaux is excellent at all price levels.*

Moreno Wines

11 Marylands Road, London W9 2DU (020) 7286 0678 **fax** (020) 7286 0513 **email** merchant@moreno-wines.co.uk **website** www.morenowinedirect.com **hours** Mon–Fri 4–8, Sat 12–8 **cards** AmEx, Maestro, MasterCard, Visa **discounts** 10% on 1 or more cases **delivery** Up to 1 case £8, up to 2 cases £10, free thereafter. **M T**
✪ *Specialist in Spanish wines, from everyday drinking to fine and rare wines from older vintages, with a few well-chosen additions from Australia, Italy and elsewhere.*

Wm Morrisons Supermarkets

head office Hilmore House, Gain Lane, Bradford, West Yorkshire BD3 7DL 0845 611 5000 **fax** 0845 611 6801; 478 licensed branches **customer service** 0845 611 6111; Mon–Fri 8–6.30, Sat 9–5 **website** www.morrisons.co.uk **hours** Variable, generally Mon–Sat 7–9, Sun 10–4 **cards** AmEx, Delta, Maestro, MasterCard, Style, Visa Electron. **G T**
✪ *Inexpensive, often tasty wines, and if you're prepared to trade up a little there's some really good stuff here.*

Naked Wines

head office The Loft, Holland Court, The Close, Norwich, NR1 4DY **enquiries** 01603 281800 **email** hello@nakedwines.com **website** www.nakedwines.com **hours** Mon–Fri, UK office hours **cards** AmEx, Delta, Maestro, MasterCard, Visa, Visa Debit **discounts** 25-50% off for Angel members **delivery** UK mainland and Northern Ireland, free delivery for orders of £75 or more to most UK postcodes. **M T**
✪ *The UK's fastest growing online retailer. They also support talented up-and-coming winemakers around the world through their Naked AWine Angel scheme.*

New Zealand House of Wine

mail order/online based near Petworth, Surrey **email** info@nzhouseofwine.com **website** www.nzhouseofwine.co.uk **order freephone** 0800 085 6273 **enquiries** (01428) 70 77 33 fax (01428) 70 77 66 **hours** Mon–Fri, UK office hours **cards** AmEx, Delta, Maestro, MasterCard, Visa, Visa Debit **discounts** often available on high-volume orders (60+ bottles) for parties, weddings and other events **delivery** UK mainland only: free delivery for orders above £200, £5.99 for orders above £100, £9.59 for orders less than £100. **M**
✪ *Impressive list of over 300 New Zealand wines, with plenty under £10 and some really fine stuff around £20 and over.*

James Nicholson

7/9 Killyleagh Street, Crossgar, Co. Down, Northern Ireland BT30 9DQ (028) 4483 0091 **fax** (028) 4483 0028 **email** shop@jnwine.com **website** www.jnwine.com **hours** Mon–Sat 10–7 **cards** Maestro, MasterCard, Visa **discounts** 10% mixed case **delivery** Free (1 case or more) in R.O.I. and Northern Ireland; UK mainland £10.95, 2 cases £15.95 **en primeur** Bordeaux, Burgundy, California, Rioja, Rhône. **C G M T**
✪ *Well-chosen list mainly from small, committed growers around the world. Bordeaux, Rhône and southern France are slightly ahead of the field and there's a good selection of Burgundy and some excellent drinking from Germany and Spain.*

Nickolls & Perks

37 Lower High Street, Stourbridge, West Midlands DY8 1TA (01384) 394518
fax (01384) 440786 **email** sales@nickollsandperks.co.uk **website** www.nickollsandperks.co.uk **hours** Tues–Fri 10.30–5.30, Sat 10.30–5 **cards** Maestro, MasterCard, Visa
discounts negotiable per case **delivery** £10 per consignment; free over £150
en primeur Bordeaux, Champagne, Port. **C G M T**
✪ *Established in 1797, Nickolls & Perks has a wide-ranging list – and a terrific website – covering most areas. Its strength is France. Advice is available to clients wishing to develop their cellars or invest in wine.*

Nidderdale Fine Wines

2a High Street, Pateley Bridge, North Yorkshire, HG3 5AW (01423) 711703
email mike@southaustralianwines.com **website** www.southaustralianwines.com
hours Tues–Sat 10–6 **cards** Maestro, MasterCard, Visa **discounts** 5% case discount on shop purchases for 12+ bottles **delivery** £5 per 12-bottle case in England, Wales and southern Scotland. Single bottle delivery available. **G M T**
✪ *Specialist in South Australia, with around 300 wines broken down into regions. Also 350 or so wines from the rest of the world. Look out for online offers and winemaker dinners.*

Noble Rot Wine Warehouses

Willowbrook Garden Centre, 222 Stourbridge Road, Catfield, Bromsgrove, Worcestershire
B61 0BW (01527) 758232 **email** info@noble-rot.co.uk **website** www.noble-rot.co.uk
hours Mon–Sat 10.30–5 **cards** Maestro, MasterCard, Visa **discounts** Various
delivery Free within 10-mile radius. **G T**
✪ *Australia, Italy, France and Spain feature strongly in a frequently changing array of more than 400 wines, mostly at £10–£15. Also a selection of fine wines and Champagnes.*

O'Briens

head office 33 Spruce Avenue, Stillorgan Industrial Park, Co. Dublin, Ireland 1850 269 777;
fax 01 269 7480; 32 stores in Ireland **email** sales@obrienswines.ie; info@obrienswines.ie
website www.wine.ie **hours** Mon–Sat 10.30–10, Sun 12.30–10 **cards** AmEx, MasterCard,
Visa **delivery** €7.99 delivery anywhere in Ireland (no minimum order); free for orders over
€60 **en primeur** Bordeaux. **G M T**
✪ *Family-owned drinks retailer, which could well claim to be the best of the chains in Ireland. Imports directly from over 75 wineries worldwide.*

Old Butcher's Wine Cellar

High Street, Cookham, Berkshire SL6 9SQ (01628) 643510
email nigel@oldbutcherswinecellar.co.uk **website** www.oldbutcherswinecellar.co.uk
hours Tues–Thurs 10–6.30 Fri–Sat 10–7 **cards** Switch, Maestro, MasterCard, Visa
delivery Mainland England, Wales and southern Scotland: £5.99 per case of 12, £9.99 for under 12 bottles **G M T**
✪ *The emphasis here is on producers from the New World as well as modern European ones. Over 400 different wines in stock.*

Old Chapel Cellars

The Old Chapel, Millpool, Truro, Cornwall TR1 1EX (01872) 270545
email jamie@oldchapelcellars.co.uk **website** www.oldchapelcellars.co.uk
hours Mon–Sat 10–6 **cards** Maestro, MasterCard, Visa **delivery** £7.99 per case UK
mainland; free for orders over £95. **G M T**
✪ *Excellent, knowledgeable list that specializes in Spain and Portugal, plus wines from all over the world.*

The Oxford Wine Company

The Wine Warehouse, Witney Road, Standlake, Oxfordshire OX29 7PR (01865) 301144
fax (01865) 301155 **email** orders@oxfordwine.co.uk **website** www.oxfordwine.co.uk
hours Mon–Sat 9–7 **cards** AmEx, Diners, Maestro, MasterCard, Visa **discounts** 5% discount
on a case of 12 **delivery** Free locally; national delivery £9.99 for any amount
en primeur Bordeaux. **G M T**
• 165 Botley Road, Oxford OX2 0PB (01865) 249500 **hours** Mon–Sat 10–8, Sun 11–4
• Units 1 & 2, Baytree Court, The Chippings, Tetbury, Gloucestershire GL8 8ET
(01666) 500429 **hours** Mon–Sat 10–6.30
• 20 West Way, Cirencester, Gloucester GL7 1JA (01285) 659792 **hours** Mon-Sat 10-7,
Sun 11-4
✪ *Award-winning independent wine merchant selling a good selection of wines from the classic regions and the New World, from bargain basement prices to expensive fine wines. Plenty of tasting events on offer, too.*

OZ WINES

mail order Oz Wines, Freepost RSHB-HHTE-CZGH, Berkshire SL6 5AQ (0845)
4501261 **email** sales@ozwines.co.uk **website** www.ozwines.co.uk **hours** Mon–Fri
8–6 **cards** Almost all major credit cards **delivery** Free **minimum order** 1 mixed case. **M T**
✪ *Australian wines made by small wineries and real people – with the thrilling flavours that Australians do better than anyone.*

Penistone Wine Cellars

The Railway Station, Penistone, Sheffield, South Yorkshire S36 6HP (01226) 766037
email orders@pcwine.plus.com **website** www.penistonewines.co.uk **hours** Tues–Fri 10–6,
Sat 10–3 **cards** Maestro, MasterCard, Visa **delivery** Free locally, rest of UK mainland
charged at cost **minimum order** No minimum order **G M**
✪ *A well-balanced list, with something from just about everywhere, mostly from familiar names. Two good English fizzes: Coates & Seely and Nyetimber.*

Philglas & Swiggot

21 Northcote Road, Battersea, London SW11 1NG (020) 7924 4494
email info@philglas-swiggot.co.uk **website** www.philglas-swiggot.com
hours Mon–Sat 11–7, Sun 12–5 **cards** AmEx, Maestro, MasterCard, Visa
discounts 5% per case **delivery** Free 1 case locally, or £5 elsewhere. **G M**
• 64 Hill Rise, Richmond, London TW10 6UB (020) 8332 6031
• 22 New Quebec Street, Marylebone, London W1H 7SB (020) 7402 0002

✪ *Excellent selections from Australia, Italy, France and Austria – interesting, characterful wines rather than blockbuster brands. Subscriber's club with estate wines, bin ends and limited allocation wines.*

Christopher Piper Wines
1 Silver Street, Ottery St Mary, Devon EX11 1DB (01404) 814139 **fax** (01404) 812100
email sales@christopherpiperwines.co.uk **website** www.christopherpiperwines.co.uk
hours Mon–Fri 8.30–5.30, Sat 9–4.30 **cards** Maestro, MasterCard, Visa
discounts 5% mixed case, 10% 3 or more cases **delivery** £9.20 for 1 case then £4.90 for each case, free delivery within van areas and for orders over £220 inc VAT
en primeur Bordeaux, Burgundy, Rhône. **C G M T**
✪ *Huge range of well-chosen wines that reflect a sense of place and personality, with lots of information to help you make up your mind.*

Planet of the Grapes
shop 9 New Oxford Street, Holborn, WC1A 1BA, 020 7405 4912
wine bars • 9/10 Bulls Head Passage, Leadenhall Market, EC3V 1LU, 020 7929 7224
• 74-82 Queen Victoria Street, Bow Lane, EC4N 4SJ, 020 7248 1892
email sales@planetofthegrapes.co.uk **website** www.planetofthegrapes.co.uk
enquiries 020 7405 4912 **hours** Mon 10–6, Tues–Fri 10–7 **cards** AmEx, Delta, Maestro, MasterCard, Visa, Visa Debit **discounts** 10% off cases of 12 or more **delivery** UK mainland only: free delivery for orders of £75 or more to London. **M**
✪ *New wine shop in Holborn offering a wide range of wines (including my top white wine this year, an Australian Chardonnay, see page 20), tasting events and wine dinners, plus 2 wine bars.*

Terry Platt Wine Merchants See Tanners.

Portland Wine Company
152a Ashley Road, Hale, Altrincham, Cheshire WA15 9SA (0161) 928 0357
fax (0161) 905 1291 **email** info@portlandwine.co.uk **website** www.portlandwine.
co.uk **hours** Mon–Fri 10–9, Sat 9–9 **cards** Maestro, MasterCard, Visa **discounts** 5% on 2 cases or more, 10% on 5 cases or more **delivery** Free for orders over £100 per consignment nationwide, smaller orders at a cost. **en primeur** Bordeaux. **C T**
• 54 London Road, Alderley Edge, Cheshire SK5 7DX (01625) 590919
• 82 Chester Road, Macclesfield, Cheshire SK11 8DA (01625) 616147
• 45–47 Compstall Road, Marple Bridge, Cheshire SK6 5HG (0161) 4260155
• 44 High Street, Tarporley, Cheshire CW6 0DX (01829) 730762
✪ *Spain, Portugal and Burgundy are specialities and there's a promising-looking list of clarets. Consumer-friendly list with something at every price level from around the world.*

Private Cellar
mail order 51 The Estate Office, Kentford Lodge, Kentford, Newmarket, Suffolk CB8 7QS
(01353) 721999 **fax** (01353) 724074 **email** orders@privatecellar.co.uk
website www.privatecellar.co.uk **hours** Mon–Fri 8–6 **cards** Delta, Maestro, MasterCard, Visa **delivery** £14.50, or free for orders of 24+ bottles in mainland England and Wales.

For Scotland, islands, Northern Ireland and worldwide, phone for quote
en primeur Bordeaux, Burgundy, Rhône, Germany, Port, California. **C M T**
✪ *Friendly, personal wine advice is part of the service; wines are predominantly French, with lots of 'everyday claret' at £10–£15.*

Quaff Fine Wine Merchant

139–141 Portland Road, Hove BN3 5QJ (01273) 820320 **fax** (01273) 820326
email sales@quaffit.com **website** www.quaffwine.com **hours** Mon–Sat 9–9, Sun 10–9
cards Access, Maestro, MasterCard, Visa **discounts** 10% mixed case
delivery Next working day nationwide, charge depends on order value. **C G M T**
• Quaff 2 Ltd, 5 King's Parade, Ditchling Road, Brighton BN1 6JT 01273 553353
hours Sun–Thur 10–9, Fri–Sat 10–10 **email** fiveways@quaffit.com
✪ *Extensive and keenly priced list with no emphasis on any one country.*

Raeburn Fine Wines

21–23 Comely Bank Road, Edinburgh EH4 1DS (0131) 343 1159 **fax** (0131) 332 5166
email sales@raeburnfinewines.com **website** www.raeburnfinewines.com
hours Mon–Sat 10–6 **cards** AmEx, Maestro, MasterCard, Visa **discounts** 5% unsplit case,
2.5% mixed case **delivery** Free local area 1 or more cases (usually); elsewhere at cost
en primeur Australia, Bordeaux, Burgundy, California, Germany, Italy, Languedoc-
Roussillon, Loire, New Zealand, Rhône. **G M T**
✪ *Carefully chosen list, mainly from small growers. Italy and France – especially Burgundy – are specialities, with Germany, Austria and northern Spain close behind, as well as selected Port and sought-after California wines such as Shafer Vineyards and Turley Cellars.*

The Real Wine Company

mail order c/o Pinewood Nurseries, Wexham Street, Stoke Poges, Buckinghamshire SL3
6NB (01753) 664190 **email** mark@therealwineco.co.uk
website www.therealwineco.co.uk **cards** Delta, Maestro, MasterCard, Visa, AmEx
delivery £6.99 per order, orders over £250 free **minimum order** 1 mixed case.
✪ *Owner Mark Hughes has based his list entirely on his personal taste – check it out and see if you agree with his lively tasting notes. Plenty of good-value wines. There are also wine and food matches, with recipe suggestions.*

Reid Wines

The Mill, Marsh Lane, Hallatrow, Nr Bristol BS39 6EB (01761) 452645
fax (01761) 453642 **email** reidwines@aol.com **hours** Mon–Fri 9–5.30 **cards** Access,
Maestro, MasterCard, Visa **delivery** Free within 25 miles of Hallatrow (Bristol), and in
central London for orders over 2 cases **en primeur** Claret. **C G M T**
✪ *A mix of great old wines, some old duds and splendid current stuff. Italy, USA, Australia, Port and Madeira look tremendous.*

Reserve Wines

176 Burton Road, West Didsbury, Manchester M20 1LH (0161) 438 0101
email sales@reservewines.co.uk **website** www.reservewines.co.uk **hours** Mon–Fri 12–9,
Sat 11–9, Sun 12–7 **cards** Delta, Maestro, MasterCard, Solo, Switch, Visa
delivery Starts from £8.50. **G M T**
✪ *Award-winning wine specialist established in 2003 and focusing on making the world of wine
accessible and fun.*

Howard Ripley

mail order 18 Madrid Road, London SW13 9PD (020) 8748 2608 **fax** (020) 8741 7244
email info@howardripley.com **website** www.howardripley.com **hours** Mon–Fri 9–6
cards Maestro, MasterCard, Visa **delivery** Minimum charge £11.50 + VAT, free for England
and Wales on orders over £600 ex-VAT **en primeur** Burgundy, Germany, Oregon, New
Zealand, Switzerland. **C M T**
✪ *A must-have list for serious Burgundy lovers; expensive but not excessive, and including a
great backlist of older vintages. The German range is also excellent.*

Roberson

348 Kensington High Street, London W14 8NS (020) 7371 2121 **fax** (020) 7371 4010
email enquiries@roberson.co.uk **website** www.robersonwinemerchant.co.uk;
www.roberson.co.uk **hours** Mon–Sat 10–8, Sun 12–6 **cards** Access, AmEx, Maestro,
MasterCard, Visa **discounts** Up to a third of unsplit cases, 10% mixed cases
delivery Free delivery in the UK on orders over £200, otherwise charges apply
en primeur Bordeaux, Port. **C G M T**
✪ *Fine and rare wines, sold by the bottle. All of France is excellent; so is Italy and Port. With
friendly, knowledgeable staff, the shop is well worth a visit.*

The RSJ Wine Company

33 Coin Street, London SE1 9NR (020) 7928 4554 **email** tom.king@rsj.uk.com
website www.rsj.uk.com **hours** Mon–Fri 9–6, answering machine at other times
cards AmEx, Maestro, MasterCard, Visa **delivery** Free central London, minimum 1 case;
England and Wales (per case), £15.50 1 case, £9.75 2 cases, £8.75 3-5 cases. **G M T**
✪ *A roll-call of great Loire names.*

SA Wines Online

head office/warehouse 15 Windsor Park, 50 Windsor Avenue, Merton, London SW19 2TJ
0845 456 2365 **fax** 0845 456 2366 **email** customers@sawinesonline.co.uk
website www.sawinesonline.co.uk **hours** Mon–Fri 9–5.30 **cards** AmEx, Maestro,
MasterCard, Visa **delivery** £6.99 per delivery address in UK mainland; check website
for charges to Isle of Wight, Scottish highlands and islands, Northern Ireland
minimum order 1 mixed case **discounts** £10 off first order (over £60); loyalty scheme. **M T**
✪ *Your first stop for South African wines in the UK – and if they don't list the wine you want,
they may still be able to help you get it. The website is full of information on South Africa's wine
regions and producers, plus food and wine matching. Occasional warehouse tastings
and events.*

Sainsbury's
head office 33 Holborn, London EC1N 2HT (020) 7695 6000 **customer service** 0800 636262;
1000 stores **website** www.sainsburys.co.uk **online groceries helpline** 0800 328 1700
hours Variable, some 24 hrs, locals Mon–Sat 7–11, Sun 10 or 11–4 **cards** AmEx, Maestro,
MasterCard, Visa **discounts** 5% for 6 bottles or more. **G M T**
✪ *A collection to cater for bargain hunters as well as lovers of good-value wine higher up the
scale. They've expanded their Taste the Difference range and got some top producers on board.*

The Sampler
266 Upper Street, London N1 2UQ (020) 7226 9500 **fax** (020) 7226 6555
email jamie@thesampler.co.uk **website** www.thesampler.co.uk **hours** Mon–Sat 11.30–9,
Sun 11.30-7 **cards** Maestro, MasterCard, Visa **delivery** Free to UK mainland for any order
over £100. Next day and Sat deliveries at extra cost **discounts** 10% for 6 bottles or more, or
to online orders over £100. **G M T**
• 35 Thurloe Place, London SW7 2HP (020) 7225 5091 **hours** Mon–Sat 11.30–10, Sun
11.30-7
✪ *The future of wine retailing? 1200 wines (strengths include older vintages of Bordeaux and
Rioja, Sherry and grower Champagnes), long opening hours, email newsletters and sampling
machines allowing you to taste up to 80 wines before buying. Regular tastings and courses.*

Savage Selection
The Ox House, Market Place, Northleach, Cheltenham, Glos GL54 3EG (01451) 860896
fax (01451) 860996 **website** www.savageselection.co.uk **hours** Office Mon–Fri 9-6; shop
and wine bar Tue–Sat 10–10 cards Maestro, MasterCard, Visa **delivery** Free locally for
orders over £100; elsewhere on UK mainland free for orders over £250; smaller orders £10
+ VAT for 1 case and £5 + VAT for each additional case **en primeur** Bordeaux. **C G M T**
• The Ox House Shop and Wine Bar at same address (01451) 860680 **email** wine@
savageselection.co.uk
✪ *Owner Mark Savage MW seeks out wines of genuine originality and personality from small
family estates. France is the mainstay, alongside wines from Slovenia, Oregon and elsewhere.*

Seckford Wines
Dock Lane, Melton, Suffolk IP12 1PE (01394) 446622 **fax** (01394) 446633
email sales@seckfordwines.co.uk **website** www.seckfordwines.co.uk **cards** Maestro,
MasterCard, Visa **delivery** £18.00 per consignment in UK mainland; elsewhere at cost
minimum order 1 mixed case **en primeur** Bordeaux, Burgundy. **C M**
✪ *Bordeaux, Burgundy, Champagne and the Rhône are the stars of this list, with some
excellent older vintages. Serious stuff from Italy and Spain, too.*

Selfridges
400 Oxford Street, London W1A 1AB 0800 123 400 (for all stores)
hours London Mon–Sat 9.30–8.30, Sun 12–6 **email** wineshop@selfridges.co.uk
website www.selfridges.co.uk **cards** AmEx, Maestro, MasterCard, Visa
discounts 10% case discount **delivery** £10 within 3 working days, UK mainland. **T**

• Upper Mall East, Bullring, Birmingham B5 4BP **hours** Mon–Fri 10–8 (Thur 10–9), Sat 9–8, Sun 11–5
• 1 Exchange Square, Manchester M3 1BD
• The Trafford Centre, Manchester M17 8DA **hours** both Manchester branches Mon–Fri 10–8 (Thur 10–9), Sat 9–8, Sun 11–5
✪ *Strong fine wine list with a wide range of classics, from Bordeaux through to Tokaji from Hungary. As well as less expensive bottles, there are plenty of highly sought-after wines at £500-plus. Regular tastings.*

Slurp
head office Park Royal, London **email** info@slurp.co.uk
website www.slurp.co.uk **enquiries** 0844 544 5464 **hours** Mon–Fri, UK office hours
cards AmEx, Delta, Maestro, MasterCard, Visa, Visa Debit **discounts** £20 off first order **delivery** UK mainland £5.95, Europe and international available. **M**
✪ *Online retailer with over 5000 wines, beers and spirits to choose from. Helpful categories such as Wine in singles, Lower alchohol wines and Daily deals with over 80% discount.*

Somerfield *See Co-operative.*

Sommelier Wine Company
23 St George's Esplanade, St Peter Port, Guernsey, Channel Islands GY1 2BG (01481) 721677 **fax** (01481) 716818 **email** som.grapevine@cwgsy.net **hours** Mon–Sat 9.15–5.30, except Fri 9.15–6 **cards** Maestro, MasterCard, Visa **discounts** 5% 1 case or more
delivery Free locally (minimum 1 mixed case); being outside the EU and with Customs restrictions means that the shipping of wine to the UK mainland is not possible. **G T**
✪ *An excellent list, with interesting, unusual wines.*

Stainton Wines
1 Station Yard, Station Road, Kendal, Cumbria LA9 6BT (01539) 731886 **fax** (01539) 730396
email admin@stainton-wines.co.uk **website** www.stainton-wines.co.uk **hours** Mon–Fri 9–5.30, Sat 9–4.30 **cards** Maestro, MasterCard, Visa **discounts** 5% mixed case
delivery Free Cumbria and North Lancashire; elsewhere (per case) £13 for 1 case, more than 1 case variable. **G M T**
✪ *Some great Bordeaux, interesting Burgundy, and leading names from Italy and Chile.*

Stevens Garnier
47 West Way, Botley, Oxford OX2 0JF (01865) 263303 **fax** (01865) 791594
email shop@stevensgarnier.co.uk **website** www.stevensgarnier.co.uk
hours Mon–Thur 10–6, Fri 10–7, Sat 10–5 **cards** AmEx, MasterCard, Visa **discounts** 10% on 12 bottles **delivery** Free locally. **G M T**
✪ *Regional France is a strength: this is one of the few places in the UK you can buy wine from Savoie. Likewise, there are interesting choices from Portugal, Australia, Chile and Canada.*

retailers' directory

The following services are available where indicated: **C** = cellarage **G** = glass hire/loan **M** = mail/online order **T** = tastings and talks

183

Stone, Vine & Sun

mail order No. 13 Humphrey Farms, Hazeley Road, Twyford, Winchester, Hampshire SO21 1QA (01962) 712351 **fax** (01962) 717545 **email** sales@stonevine.co.uk
website www.stonevine.co.uk **hours** Mon–Fri 9–6, Sat 9.30–4 **cards** Access, Maestro, MasterCard, Visa **discounts** 5% on an unmixed case **delivery** £5.50 for 1st case, £8.50 for 2 cases, free for orders over £250. Prices vary for Scottish Highlands, islands and Northern Ireland. **G M T**
✪ *Lovely list marked by enthusiasm and passion for the subject. Lots of interesting stuff from France, especially the Rhône, Burgundy, Languedoc-Roussillon and the Loire. South Africa and South America are other strong areas, plus there are wines from Germany, New Zealand, the USA and elsewhere.*

Sunday Times Wine Club

mail order New Aquitaine House, Exeter Way, Theale, Reading, Berkshire RG7 4PL
order line 0845 217 9122 **fax** 0845 217 9144 **email** orders@sundaytimeswineclub. co.uk **website** www.sundaytimeswineclub.co.uk **hours** Mon–Fri 8.30–9, Sat–Sun 9–6 **cards** AmEx, Diners, Maestro, MasterCard, Visa **delivery** £5.99 per order
en primeur Australia, Bordeaux, Burgundy, Rhône. **C M T**
✪ *Essentially the same as Laithwaites (see page 173). The Club runs tours and tasting events for its members.*

Swig

mail order/online 188 Sutton Court Road, London W4 3HR (020) 8995 7060 or freephone 08000 272 272 **fax** (020) 8995 6195 **email** wine@swig.co.uk **website** www.swig.co.uk **cards** Amex, MasterCard, Switch, Visa **delivery** Free for orders over £90
en primeur Bordeaux, Burgundy, South Africa. **C G M T**
✪ *Seriously good wines sold in an unserious way. For instant recommendations there's a list of 'current favourites' organized in price bands; there's lots between £8 and £20 and the list covers pretty much everything you might want.*

T & W Wines

5 Station Way, Brandon, Suffolk IP27 0BH (01842) 814414 **fax** (01842) 819967
email contact@tw-wines.com **website** www.tw-wines.com **hours** Mon–Fri 9–5.30, occasional Sat 9.30–1 **cards** AmEx, MasterCard, Visa **delivery** (Most areas) 7–23 bottles £18.95 + VAT, 2 or more cases free **en primeur** Burgundy. **C G M T**
✪ *A good list, particularly if you're looking for interesting wines from Burgundy, Rhône, Alsace or the Loire, but prices are not especially low.*

Tanners

26 Wyle Cop, Shrewsbury, Shropshire SY1 1XD (01743) 234500 **fax** (01743) 234501
hours Mon–Sat 9–6 **email** sales@tanners-wines.co.uk **website** www.tanners-wines. co.uk **cards** Maestro, MasterCard, Visa **discounts** 5% 1 mixed case, 7.5% 3 mixed cases (cash & collection); 5% for 2 mixed cases, 7.5% for 4 (mail order) **delivery** Free on orders over £90 to one address, otherwise £7.95 **en primeur** Bordeaux, Burgundy, Rhône, Germany, Port, occasionally others. **C G M T**

• 36 High Street, Bridgnorth WV16 4DB (01746) 763148 **fax** (01746) 769798
hours Mon–Sat 9–5.30
• 4 St Peter's Square, Hereford HR1 2PG (01432) 272044 **fax** (01432) 263316
hours Mon–Sat 9–5.30
• Council Street West, Llandudno LL30 1ED (01492) 874099 **fax** (01492) 874788
hours Mon–Fri 9–5.30 (formerly Terry Platt Wines)
• Severn Farm Enterprise Park, Welshpool SY21 7DF (01938) 552542 **fax** (01938) 556565
hours Mon–Fri 9–5.30, Sat 9–1
✪ *Outstanding, award-winning merchant: Bordeaux, Burgundy and Germany are terrific – and there's excellent stuff from elsewhere, as well as Port, Madeira and Sherry. Terry Platt Wines in Llandudno is now part of the Tanners empire.*

Terroir Languedoc Wines

mail order/online Treetops, Grassington Road, Skipton, North Yorkshire BD23 1LL
(01756) 700512 **fax** (01756) 797856 **email** enquiries@terroirlanguedoc.co.uk
website www.terroirlanguedoc.co.uk **hours** Mon–Fri 8:30–5:30 **cards** Maestro,
MasterCard, Visa **discount** Mixed case offers available alongside bespoke service. **M T**
✪ *Hand-picked list of wines from interesting growers in the Languedoc, one of France's most innovative wine regions.*

Tesco

head office Tesco House, PO Box 18, Delamare Road, Cheshunt EN8 9SL
(01992) 632222 **fax** (01992) 630794 **customer service** 0800 505555; 2400 licensed branches
email customer.services@tesco.co.uk **website** www.tesco.com **hours** Variable
cards Maestro, MasterCard, Visa **discounts** 5% on 6 bottles or more. **G M T**
• **online** www.tesco.com/wine **discounts** All cases include a 5% discount to match offers in-store, discounts vary monthly on featured cases **cards** AmEx, Mastercard, Visa, Maestro, Clubcard Plus **minimum order** 1 case (6 bottles), 6 bottles for Champagne **delivery** Choice of next day delivery or convenient 2-hour slots
✪ *A range of 850 wines from everyday drinking to fine wines. Tesco.com/wine has an even greater selection by the case. New features include fine wine and a next day delivery system.*

House of Townend

Wyke Way, Melton West Business Park, Hull, East Yorkshire HU14 3HH (01482) 638888
email sales@houseoftownend.co.uk **website** www.houseoftownend.com **hours** (Cellar door) Mon– Fri 9.00-6.30 , Sat 9.00-1.00 **cards** AmEx, Maestro, MasterCard, Visa
discounts 5% per case **delivery** Free 1 case locally, or £5 elsewhere. **C G M T**
✪ *Solid range at all price points, with some mature wines from the classic European areas.*

Turville Valley Wines

The Firs, Potter Row, Great Missenden, Bucks HP16 9LT (01494) 868818 **fax** (01494) 866680
email chris@turville-valley-wines.com **website** www.turville-valley-wines.com
hours Mon–Fri 9–5.30 **cards** None **delivery** By arrangement **minimum order** £300
excluding VAT/12 bottles. **C M**
✪ *Top-quality fine and rare wines at trade prices.*

Vagabond

18-22 Vanston Place, London SW6 1AX (020) 7381 1717
email info@vagabondwines.co.uk **website** www.vagabondwines.co.uk
hours Mon–Fri 12–9, Sat 11–9, Sun 11–8 **cards** Visa, MasterCard, Amex **discounts** 6% off
any mixed six, 12% off any mixed dozen. **delivery** free within a 2-mile radius and UK orders
over £250 **minimum order** 6 bottles or more. **G M T**
✪ *New, award-winning retailer. A carefully chosen selection of 150–200 wines which you can
taste before you buy, from 50p a sample. The wines are listed by style rather than by country.*

Valvona & Crolla

19 Elm Row, Edinburgh EH7 4AA (0131) 556 6066 **fax** (0131) 556 1668
email wine@valvonacrolla.co.uk **website** www.valvonacrolla.co.uk **hours** Shop: Mon–
Sat 8.30–6, Sun 10.30–4, Caffe bar: Mon–Sat 8.30–5.30, Sun 10.30–3.30 **cards** AmEx,
MasterCard, Visa **discounts** 7% 1–36 bottles, 10% 37+ bottles **delivery** Edinburgh: Free
min £30. UK: Free on orders over £150, otherwise £10; Sat mornings free on orders over
£200, otherwise £30. **M T**
✪ *Exciting selection of wines from all over the world, but specializing in Italy. 25 different Italian
liqueurs and grappas. Branches in Jenners, Edinburgh and Jenners, Loch Lomond.*

Villeneuve Wines

1 Venlaw Court, Peebles EH45 8AE (01721) 722500 **fax** (01721) 729922
email wines@villeneuvewines.com **website** www.villeneuvewines.com
hours (Peebles) Mon–Sat 10–8, Sun 12–5.30; (Haddington) Mon–Sat 10–7; (Edinburgh) Mon–
Wed 12–10, Thur–Sat 10–10, Sun 12–10 **cards** AmEx, Maestro, MasterCard, Visa
delivery Free locally, £8.50 per case elsewhere. **G M T**
• 49A Broughton Street, Edinburgh EH1 3RJ (0131) 558 8441
✪ *Italy, Australia and New Zealand are all marvellous here. France is good and Spain is clearly
an enthusiasm, too.*

Vin du Van

mail order Colthups, The Street, Appledore, Kent TN26 2BX (01233) 758727
fax (01233) 758389 **website** www.vinduvan.co.uk **hours** Mon–Fri 9–5 **cards** Delta, Maestro,
MasterCard, Visa **delivery** Free locally; elsewhere £7.95 for 1st case, further cases free.
For Highlands and islands, ask for quote **minimum order** 1 mixed case. **M**
✪ *Extensive, wonderfully quirky, star-studded Australian list, one of the best in the UK; the kind
of inspired lunacy I'd take to read on a desert island.*

Vinceremos

mail order Royal House, Sovereign Street, Leeds LS1 4BJ (0800) 107 3086
fax (0113) 288 4566 **email** info@vinceremos.co.uk **website** www.vinceremos.co.uk
hours Mon–Fri 9–5.30 **cards** AmEx, Delta, Maestro, MasterCard, Visa **discounts** 5% on
5 cases or more, 10% on 10 cases or more **delivery** Free 5 cases or more. **G M**
✪ *Organic specialist, with a wide-ranging list of wines, including biodynamic and Fairtrade.
In addition to wine, you can buy fruit wine, beer, cider and perry, spirits and liqueurs.*

Vini Italiani

72 Old Brompton Road, London SW7 3LQ (020) 7225 2283 **fax** (020) 7225 0848
email info@vini-italiani.co.uk **website** www.vini-italiani.co.uk **hours** Mon–Sat 10–10, Sun
11–7 **cards** AmEx, Maestro, MasterCard, Visa **delivery** Free local delivery, cheap London
delivery and standard delivery charge for mainland UK **minimum order** 1 case. **C G T**
✪ *Exciting new Italy-only store with fascinating range of classic and non-classic wines.*
Enomatic sampling machines, courses,masterclasses and plenty more.

Vinoteca

7 Saint John Street, London EC1M 4AA (020) 7253 8786
email farringdon@vinoteca.co.uk **hours** Mon–Sat 11 to 11, Sunday 11 to 5 (except
Farringdon) **email** wineshop@vinoteca.co.uk **website** www.vinoteca.co.uk
cards AmEx, Maestro, MasterCard, Visa, **discounts** 5% for 12 bottles or more
collected **delivery** Free for orders over £150, UK excluding Scottish highlands and
islands, **minimum order** 1 bottle. **M T**
• Marylebone 15 Seymour Place, London W1H 5BD (020) 7724 7288
email marylebone@vinoteca.co.uk
• Soho 53-55 Beak Street, London W1F 9SH (020) 3544 7411 **email** soho@vinoteca.co.uk
✪ *Established in 2005 Vinoteca now has three wine bars cum restaurants cum shops offering a*
good range of wines, plus wine tastings and themed dinners. Unstuffy, lively places to buy, taste
and learn about wine.

Vintage Roots

mail order Holdshott Farm, Reading Road, Heckfield, Hook, Hampshire RG27 0JZ
(0118) 932 6566, (0800) 980 4992 **fax** (0118) 922 5115 **hours** Mon–Fri 8.30–5.30, Sat in
December **email** info@vintageroots.co.uk **website** www.vintageroots.co.uk **cards** Delta,
Maestro, MasterCard, Visa **discounts** 5% on 5 cases or over **delivery** Free for orders over
£250 and £6.95 for all orders under £250. **G M T**
✪ *Everything on this list of over 300 wines is certified organic and/or biodynamic. As well as*
wine, Vintage Roots sells organic beer, cider, liqueurs and spirits, and chocolate at Christmas
time.

Virgin Wines

mail order/online The Loft, St James' Mill, Whitefriars, Norwich NR3 1TN
0843 224 1001 **fax** (01603) 619277 **email** help@virginwines.co.uk
website www.virginwines.co.uk **hours** (Office) Mon–Fri 8–8, Sat–Sun 9–6
cards AmEx, Maestro, MasterCard, Visa, Paypal **delivery** £6.99 per order for all
UK deliveries **minimum order** 1 case. **M T**
✪ *Well-established online retailer. Reasonably priced wines from all over the world.*
Additional features include a Wine Bank to help you save for your next case and online auctions.

Waitrose

head office Doncaster Road, Southern Industrial Area, Bracknell, Berkshire
RG12 8YA **customer service** 0800 188884, 279 licensed stores

email customersupport@waitrose.co.uk **website** www.waitrosewine.com
hours See www.waitrose.com for branch opening hours **cards** AmEx, Delta, Maestro,
MasterCard, Partnership Card, Visa **discounts** Regular monthly promotions, 5% off for 6
bottles or more **home delivery** Available through www.waitrose.com and www.ocado.com
and Waitrose Wine Direct (below) **en primeur** Bordeaux and Burgundy available through
Waitrose Wine Direct. **G M T**
• **waitrose wine direct** order online at www.waitrosewine.com or 0800 188881
discounts Vary monthly on featured cases; branch promotions are matched. All cases
include a 5% discount to match branch offer. **delivery** Free standard delivery throughout
UK mainland, Northern Ireland and Isle of Wight. Named day delivery, £6.95 per addressee
(order by 6pm for next day – not Sun); next-day delivery before 10.30am, £9.95 per
addressee (order by 6pm for next working day).
❂ *Ahead of the other supermarkets in quality, value and imagination. Still lots of tasty stuff
under £6.*

Waterloo Wine Co
office and warehouse 6 Vine Yard, London SE1 1QL **shop** 59–61 Lant Street, London SE1
1QN (020) 7403 7967 **fax** (020) 7357 6976 **email** sales@waterloowine.co.uk
website www.waterloowine.co.uk **hours** Mon–Fri 11–7.30, Sat 10–5 **cards** AmEx, Maestro,
MasterCard, Visa **delivery** Free 1 case central London; elsewhere, 1 case £12, 2 cases
£7.50 each. **G T**
❂ *Quirky, personal list, strong in the Loire and New Zealand.*

Weald Wine Cellars
Moor Hill, Hawkhurst, Kent TN18 4PF (01580) 753487 **fax** (01580) 755627
email kvgriffin@aol.com **website** www.maison-du-vin.co.uk **hours** Mon 10–4, Tue–Fri
10–5, Sat 10–6 **cards** Access, AmEx, Maestro, MasterCard, Visa **delivery** Free locally; UK
mainland at cost **en primeur** Bordeaux. **C G M T**
❂ *Previously known as Maison du Vin, now owned by Weald Wine Cellars. The focus is on
French wines, and interesting wines, not brands. There is some good stuff from Australia and
Chile – at prices from about £6 upwards. There's a monthly themed 'wine school' and you can
book personal tutored tastings.*

Wimbledon Wine Cellar
1 Gladstone Road, Wimbledon, London SW19 1QU (020) 8540 9979 **fax** (020) 8540 9399
email enquiries@wimbledonwinecellar.com **hours** Mon–Sat 10–9
website www.wimbledonwinecellar.com **cards** AmEx, Maestro, MasterCard, Visa
discounts 10% off 1 case (with a few exceptions), 20% off case of 6 Champagne
delivery Free local delivery. Courier charges elsewhere **en primeur** Burgundy, Bordeaux,
Tuscany, Rhône. **C G M T**
• 4 The Boulevard, Imperial Wharf, Chelsea, London SW6 2UB (020) 7736 2191
email chelsea@wimbledonwinecellar.com **hours** Mon–Sat 10–9, Sun 11–7
❂ *Top names from Italy, Burgundy, Bordeaux, Rhône, Loire – and some of the best producers of
the New World.*

Wine & Beer World (Majestic)

head office Majestic House, Otterspool Way, Watford, Hertfordshire WD25 8WW
(01923) 298200 **email** info@wineandbeer.co.uk **website** www.majesticinfrance.co.uk
pre-order (01923) 298297 **discounts** Available for large pre-orders
cards Maestro, MasterCard, Visa. **T**
• Rue du Judée, Zone Marcel Doret, Calais 62100, France (00 33) 3 21 97 63 00
email calais@majestic.co.uk **hours** 7 days 8–8, including bank holidays
• Centre Commercial Carrefour, Quai L'Entrepôt, Cherbourg 50100, France
(00 33) 2 33 22 23 22 **email** cherbourg@majestic.co.uk **hours** Mon–Sat 9–7
• Unit 3A, Zone La Française, Coquelles 62331, France (00 33) 3 21 82 93 64
email coquelles@majestic.co.uk **hours** 7 days 9–7, including bank holidays
✪ *The French arm of Majestic, with 300 wines at least £2 less per bottle than Majestic UK prices. Calais is the largest branch and Coquelles the nearest to the Channel Tunnel terminal. English-speaking staff.*

The Wine Company (Devon)

mail order Town Barton, Doddiscombsleigh, Nr Exeter, Devon EX6 7PT
(01647) 252005 **email** nick@thewinecompany.biz **website** www.thewinecompany.biz
hours Mon–Sun 9–6 **cards** Maestro, MasterCard, Visa **delivery** £8.99 per case, free for orders over £150, UK mainland only. **M**
✪ *The list of around 250 wines specializes in Australia and South Africa, with some top names you won't find anywhere else.*

The Wine Company (Essex)

Gosbecks Park, Colchester, Essex CO2 9JT (01206) 713560 **fax** (01206) 713515
email sales@thewinecompany.co.uk **website** www.thewinecompany.co.uk
hours Mon–Sat 9–6 **cards** Delta, Electron, MasterCard, Maestro, Switch, Visa
delivery free for any 12-bottle order; please ring or email for quote for Highlands, islands and Northern Ireland. **C G M T**
✪ *Family-owned wine merchant, strong in French wines and wines from smaller estates, with plenty under £10. Well-chosen mixed case offers and regular tastings and dinners.*

Wine Pantry

1 Stoney Street, Borough Market, London SE1 9AA (020) 7403 3003
email info@winepantry.co.uk **website** www.winepantry.co.uk **hours** Tues–Fri 12–8, Sat 11–8 **cards** Delta, Electron, MasterCard, Maestro, Switch, Visa **delivery** UK mainland; visit the website for other delivery details, including international. **M T**
✪ *In the heart of bustling Borough Market. Extensive list of quality English still and sparkling wines, plus English cheeses and cured meats.*

retailers' directory

The following services are available where indicated: **C** = cellarage **G** = glass hire/loan **M** = mail/online order **T** = tastings and talks

189

Wine Rack

head office Venus House, Unit 3, 62 Garman Road, London N17 0UT (020) 8801 0011
fax (020) 8801 6455 **email** info@winerack.co.uk **website** www.winerack.co.uk; 20 Wine
Rack stores and more to come **hours** Mon–Sat 10–10, Sun 11–10 **cards** Maestro,
MasterCard, Visa **delivery** Free locally, some branches. **G T**
✪ *Following the 2009 collapse of First Quench (aka Thresher's and Wine Rack) a new owner
bought the Wine Rack name and revitalized a selection of stores in London, Bristol and the
Home Counties.*

The Wine Society

mail order/online Gunnels Wood Road, Stevenage, Herts SG1 2BG (01438) 741177
fax (01438) 761167 **order line** (01438) 740222 **email** memberservices@thewinesociety.
com **website** www.thewinesociety.com **hours** Mon–Fri 8.30–9, Sat 9–5; showroom: Mon–
Fri 10–6, Thur 10–7, Sat 9.30–5.30 **cards** Delta, Maestro, MasterCard, Visa **discounts** (per
case) £3 for pre-ordered collection **delivery** Free 1 case or more anywhere in UK; also
collection facility at Templepatrick, County Antrim, and showroom and collection facility
at Montreuil, France, at French rates of duty and VAT **en primeur** Bordeaux, Burgundy,
Germany, Port, Rhône. **C G M T**
✪ *An outstanding list from an inspired wine-buying team. Masses of well-chosen, affordable
wines as well as big names. The Wine Society regularly wins the UK's top awards for wine by
mail order. Founded in 1874, The Wine Society's aim was, and remains, to introduce members to
the best of the world's vineyards at a fair price. Holding a share in The Wine Society gives you a
lifetime membership with no annual fee and no pressure to buy. The cost of a share is £40.*

The Wine Treasury

mail order 69–71 Bondway, London SW8 1SQ (020) 7793 9999 **fax** (020) 7793 8080
email bottled@winetreasury.com **website** www.winetreasury.com **hours** Mon–Fri 9.30–6
cards AmEx, Maestro, MasterCard, Visa **discounts** 10% for unmixed dozens
delivery Free for orders over £300, England and Wales; Scotland phone for more
details **minimum order** 1 mixed case. **M**
✪ *Excellent choices and top names from California and Italy – but they don't come cheap.*

Winemark the Wine Merchants

3 Duncrue Place, Belfast BT3 9BU (028) 9074 6274 **fax** (028) 9074 8022; 77 branches
email info@winemark.com **website** www.winemark.com **hours** Branches vary, but in
general Mon–Sat 10–10, Sun 12–8 **cards** Switch, MasterCard, Visa. **G T**
✪ *Over 500 wines, including some good ones from Australia, New Zealand, Chile and California.*

The Winery

4 Clifton Road, London W9 1SS (020) 7286 6475 **email** info@thewineryuk.com
website www.thewineryuk.com **hours** Mon–Sat 11–9.30, Sun and public holidays
12–8 **cards** Maestro, MasterCard, Visa **discounts** 5% on a mixed case
delivery Free locally or for 3 cases or more, otherwise £10 per case. **G M T**
✪ *Largest selection of dry German wines in the UK. Burgundy, Rhône, Champagne, Italy and
California are other specialities.*

WoodWinters

16 Henderson Street, Bridge of Allan, Scotland FK9 4HP (01786) 834894
email shop@woodwinters.com **website** www.woodwinters.com **hours** Mon–Sat 10–7;
Sun 1–5 **cards** MasterCard, Switch, Visa **discounts** Vintners Dozen: buy 12 items or
more and get a 13th free (non-alcoholic) **delivery** £8.95 per address; free for orders over
£150 UK mainland. Islands and Northern Ireland, phone for quote **en primeur** Bordeaux,
Burgundy, Italy, Rhone. **C G M T**
• 91 Newington Road, Edinburgh EH9 1QW (0131) 667 2760
✪ *A young, ambitious operation, very strong on California and Australia, but also good stuff
from Austria, Portugal, Italy, Spain and Burgundy. They do like flavour, so expect most of their
wines to be mouth-filling. Wine-tasting club and courses.*

Wright Wine Co

The Old Smithy, Raikes Road, Skipton, North Yorkshire BD23 1NP (0800) 328 4435
fax (01756) 798580 **email** enquiries@wineandwhisky.co.uk **website** www.wineandwhisky.
co.uk **hours** Mon–Fri 9–6; Sat 10–5:30; open Sundays in December 11–3 **cards** Maestro,
MasterCard, Visa **discounts** 10% unsplit case, 5% mixed case **delivery** Free within 30
miles, elsewhere at cost. **G**
✪ *Equally good in both Old World and New World, with plenty of good stuff at keen prices. Wide
choice of half-bottles.*

Peter Wylie Fine Wines

Plymtree Manor, Plymtree, Cullompton, Devon EX15 2LE (01884) 277555 **fax** (01884) 277557
email peter@wyliefinewines.co.uk **website** www.wyliefinewines.co.uk **hours** Mon–Fri
9–5.30 **discounts** Only on unsplit cases **delivery** Up to 3 cases in London £30, otherwise by
arrangement. **M**
✪ *Fascinating list of mature wines: Bordeaux from throughout the 20th century, vintage Ports
going back to the 1920s.*

Yapp Brothers

shop The Old Brewery, Water Street, Mere, Wiltshire BA12 6DY (01747) 860423
fax (01747) 860929 **email** sales@yapp.co.uk **website** www.yapp.co.uk **hours** Mon–Sat 9–6
cards Maestro, MasterCard, Visa **discounts** £6 per case on collection **delivery** free delivery
for orders over £100, otherwise £10 **C G M T**
✪ *Rhône and Loire specialists. Also some of the hard-to-find wines of Provence, Savoie,
Southwest France and Corsica, plus a small selection from Australia.*

Noel Young Wines

56 High Street, Trumpington, Cambridge CB2 9LS (01223) 566744 **fax** (01223) 844736
email admin@nywines.co.uk **website** www.nywines.co.uk **hours** Mon–Fri 10–8, Sat
10–7, Sun 12–2 **cards** AmEx, Maestro, MasterCard, Visa **discounts** 5% for orders over
£500 **delivery** Free over 12 bottles unless discounted **en primeur** Australia, Burgundy,
Italy, Rhône. **G M T**
✪ *Fantastic wines from just about everywhere. Australia is a passion and there is a great
Austrian list, some terrific Germans, plus beautiful Burgundies, Italians and dessert wines.*

who's where

COUNTRYWIDE MAIL ORDER/ ONLINE

Adnams
Aldi
Asda
AustralianWine-
  Centre
Bancroft Wines
Bibendum Wine
Big Red Wine Co
Bordeaux Index
Anthony Byrne
Cockburns of Leith
Co-op
Devigne Wines
Nick Dobson Wines
Domaine Direct
FromVineyards-
  Direct
Jeroboams
Justerini & Brooks
Laithwaites
Lay & Wheeler
Laytons
Liberty Wines
O W Loeb
Majestic
Marks & Spencer
Millésima
Montrachet
Morrisons
Naked Wines
New Zealand House
  of Wine
OZ WINES
Private Cellar
Real Wine Co
Howard Ripley
Sainsbury's
Slurp
Stone, Vine & Sun
Sunday Times Wine
  Club
Swig
Tesco
Vin du Van
Vinceremos
Vintage Roots
Virgin Wines
Waitrose
The Wine Company
The Wine Society
The Wine Treasury
Peter Wylie Fine
  Wines
Yapp Brothers
Noel Young Wines

LONDON

armit
Berkmann Wine
  Cellars
Berry Bros. & Rudd
Budgens
Corney & Barrow
Farr Vintners
Fortnum & Mason
Friarwood
Goedhuis & Co
Green & Blue
Handford Wines
Harvey Nichols
Haynes Hanson
  & Clark
Jeroboams
Lea & Sandeman
Moreno Wines
Philglas & Swiggot
Planet of the
  Grapes
Roberson
RSJ Wine Company
The Sampler
Selfridges
Vagabond
Vinoteca
Waterloo Wine Co
Wimbledon Wine
  Cellar
Wine Pantry
Wine Rack
The Winery

SOUTHEAST AND HOME COUNTIES

A&B Vintners
Berry Bros. & Rudd
Budgens
Butlers Wine Cellar
Les Caves de Pyrene
Dalling & Co.
Flagship Wines
Hedley Wright
Old Butcher's
  Wine Cellar
Quaff
Turville Valley Wines
The Wine Company
  (Essex)
Weald Wine Cellars
Wine Rack

WEST AND SOUTHWEST

Averys Wine
  Merchants
Bennetts Fine
  Wines
Berkmann Wine
  Cellars
Great Western Wine
Haynes Hanson
  & Clark
Hicks & Don
Old Chapel Cellars
Christopher Piper
  Wines
Reid Wines
Savage Selection
The Wine Company
  (Devon)

Wine Rack
Peter Wylie Fine
  Wines
Yapp Brothers

EAST ANGLIA

Adnams
Budgens
Anthony Byrne
Cambridge Wine
  Merchants
Corney & Barrow
Seckford Wines
T & W Wines
Noel Young Wines

MIDLANDS

Bat & Bottle
Connolly's
Gauntleys
Harvey Nichols
S H Jones
Nickolls & Perks
Noble Rot Wine
  Warehouses
Oxford Wine Co
Selfridges
Stevens Garnier
Tanners

NORTH

Barrica Wines
Berkmann Wine
  Cellars
Booths
D Byrne
deFINE Food and
  Wine
Halifax Wine Co
hangingditch
Harvey Nichols
Martinez Wines
Nidderdale Fine
  Wines

Penistone Wine
  Cellars
Portland Wine Co
Reserve Wines
Selfridges
Stainton Wines
Terroir Languedoc
House of Townend
Wright Wine Co

WALES

Fingal-Rock
Terry Platt (now
  part of Tanners)
Tanners

SCOTLAND

Cockburns of Leith
Corney & Barrow
Peter Green & Co
Harvey Nichols
Linlithgow Wines
Raeburn Fine Wines
Valvona & Crolla
Villeneuve Wines
WoodWinters

NORTHERN IRELAND/ IRELAND

Direct Wine
  Shipments
Harvey Nichols
James Nicholson
O'Briens
Winemark

CHANNEL ISLANDS

Sommelier Wine Co

FRANCE

Millésima
Wine & Beer World
The Wine Society